499–479 BC

COMBAT
Greek Hoplite
VERSUS
Persian Warrior

Chris McNab

Illustrated by Adam Hook

OSPREY

Bloomsbury Publishing Plc
PO Box 883, Oxford, OX1 9PL, UK
1385 Broadway, 5th Floor, New York, NY 10018, USA
E-mail: info@ospreypublishing.com
www.ospreypublishing.com

OSPREY is a trademark of Osprey Publishing Ltd

First published in Great Britain in 2018

A catalogue record for this book is available from the British Library.

ISBN: PB 9781472825742; eBook 9781472825735;
ePDF 9781472825728; XML 9781472825759

18 19 20 21 22   10 9 8 7 6 5 4 3 2 1

Maps by bounford.com
Index by Rob Munro
Typeset by PDQ Digital Media Solutions, Bungay, UK
Printed in China through World Print Ltd.

Osprey Publishing supports the Woodland Trust, the UK's leading
woodland conservation charity. Between 2014 and 2018 our donations
are being spent on their Centenary Woods project in the UK.

To find out more about our authors and books visit
www.ospreypublishing.com. Here you will find extracts, author
interviews, details of forthcoming events and the option to sign up for
our newsletter.

Artist's note

Readers may care to note that the original paintings from which the
colour plates in this book were prepared are available for private sale.
All reproduction copyright whatsoever is retained by the Publishers. All
enquiries should be addressed to:

Scorpio, 158 Mill Road, Hailsham, East Sussex BN27 2SH, UK
Email: scorpiopaintings@btinternet.com

The Publishers regret that they can enter into no correspondence upon
this matter.

Key to military symbols

Army Group	Army	Corps	Division	Brigade	Regiment	Battalion
Company/Battery	Platoon	Section	Squad	Infantry	Artillery	Cavalry
Airborne	Unit HQ	Air defence	Air Force	Air mobile	Air transportable	Amphibious
Anti-tank	Armour	Air aviation	Bridging	Engineer	Headquarters	Maintenance
Medical	Missile	Mountain	Navy	Nuclear, biological, chemical	Ordnance	Parachute
Reconnaissance	Signal	Supply	Transport movement	Fortress or static	Fortress machine gun	

Key to unit identification

Unit identifier		Parent unit
	Commander	
		(+) with added elements
		(−) less elements

CONTENTS

INTRODUCTION   **4**

THE OPPOSING SIDES   **8**
Training and service • Kit and equipment • Tactics

MARATHON   **29**
490 BC

THERMOPYLAE   **41**
480 BC

PLATAEA   **54**
479 BC

ANALYSIS   **70**

AFTERMATH   **76**

UNIT ORGANIZATIONS   **78**

BIBLIOGRAPHY   **79**

INDEX   **80**

Introduction

The story of the wars between Greeks and Persians in the 5th century BC sits on the blurred outer edges of the human narrative. Its modern narrative is put together in composite fashion, through archaeology, drama, sculpture and art, fragmentary inscriptions, but primarily through those longer works by the great figures of early historical writing: Herodotus, Xenophon, Thucydides, Plutarch and others. Taken together, the sources provide us with enough of a repository of information to patch together a reasonably informed political and military history of the Greek and Persian Wars.

Nevertheless, there remains the lingering sense that we see through a glass darkly, not least in the analysis of how the Greek and Persian warriors actually fought on the battlefield. Niche issues such as how far Greek hoplites stood apart in the phalanx, or to what extent they delivered a pushing assault against the opposing ranks, continue to strike sparks in academic and amateur historical debate. In reality, the passage of time and the incompleteness, or inaccuracy, of the sources mean that some degree of uncertainty lingers in our analysis. What we can say with reasonable certainty, however, is that the battles fought between the Greeks and the Persians between 499 and 449 BC were clashes of two quite different tactical approaches to combat, these systems being products of both cultural forces and several millennia of military development in Europe, the Middle East and Central Asia.

From the emergence of civilization – and its dark corollary, warfare – in Mesopotamia and Egypt in the 4th millennium BC, up to the 5th century BC, military forces had become structured according to two basic and still familiar types of soldier: infantry and cavalry. Infantry provided a state with military mass, a large body of armed men whose sheer numbers often compensated for a lack of ability to manoeuvre and a lack of training; many soldiers were simply agricultural workers given basic edged or impact weapons, conscripted into a seasonal campaign and pointed in

This Attic vase from the 5th or 6th century BC shows two hoplites in close-quarters combat. Note that both of the men have swung their spears up into what appear to be high overhand grips, while presenting their shields upwards to deflect downward thrusts. (DEA/A. DAGLI ORTI/ De Agostini/Getty Images)

the right direction. Furthermore, as with modern infantry, it was only the foot soldiers who could truly seize and hold territory.

Although infantry could be rather a blunt instrument, this is not to say that some formations were not well trained and highly motivated – the Egyptians, Assyrians, Sumerians, Hittites and others built broad empires through such soldiery – nor that there was not a degree of organizational and tactical sophistication. Infantry could be separated into heavy and light varieties. Heavy infantry provided *shock*, dense blocks of massed soldiers often wearing personal armour (metal or thickened fabric) and armed with spears, swords and shields, smashing into the opposing ranks and hacking and stabbing their way to a conclusion. As their lumpen label suggests, heavy infantry had limited manoeuvrability, partly because of the tactical stiffness of their close-ranked formations, partly because of their energy-depleting armour and shields, and partly because of a lack of training. Historians do, however, distinguish between 'articulated' and 'unarticulated' infantry, the former having the drill, discipline and command structures to perform unitary shifts of direction and pace, while the latter was essentially a crude linear force following its nose into action.

Light infantry, by contrast, were troops who embraced mobility, moving with more freedom and using distance to create and exploit gaps in enemy ranks and provide support to the heavy infantry. Light infantry were generally armed with missile weaponry – slings, javelins and bows – to inflict attrition and suppression from a distance, staying out of trouble themselves owing to a lack of body armour. Archers were particularly critical in this role; they provided the principal means of precision direct and indirect infantry fire for more than 5,000 years of human history.

Cavalry were the fastest arm of manoeuvre on the ancient battlefield, and were often connected with the most noble elements of an army – i.e.

those who could afford mount and equipment. Wearing varying degrees of armour, cavalry acted as mounted skirmishers or pursuit troops, firing arrows from horseback into the enemy soldiers, or conducting nimble strikes at crucial moments with sword and javelin. Together the cavalry provided the ancient armies with their most rapid means of deployment, especially in support of unarticulated infantry; a judicious application of cavalry at just the right moment could swing the outcome of a battle. Chariots, furthermore, could act as mobile missile platforms on the battlefield, with an archer or a javelineer fighting from the chariot floor while another man acted as driver.

What essentially defined one ancient army from the rest was how it combined, prioritized and weighted all the elements of its force – heavy and light infantry, archers, javelineers, charioteers, heavy and light cavalry – into a cohesive whole. The disparities in how this was achieved will be especially visible in this study. On the one side were the Greeks, their martial order focused almost exclusively on unarticulated hoplite heavy infantry. On the other side were the Persians, taking a more combined-arms approach, with a bias towards light cavalry and light infantry, a preference for movement and missiles. What happened when these different systems clashed under the hot Greek sun forms the topic of this book.

Relief from the time of the Persian king Darius I (r. 522–486 BC). It is interesting to note the variations between the figures here, some with swords, some without, and a select number having shields. As a rule, the Persians fought with a far more fluid approach to tactics than the Archaic Greeks. (Authenticated News/Archive Photos/Getty Images)

The Persian expansion into Greece, 492—490 BC

By 492 BC, the Persian Empire had swallowed up Asia Minor (having suppressed the Ionian Revolt of 499–494 BC) and was pressing against the borders of Macedonian and Greek territory from the north. In 492/491 BC, the Persian king, Darius I (r. 522–486 BC), sent envoys to the Greek states to demand obedience to the Persian Empire, and received in response a mix of compliance, indifference and outright defiance, precipitating a major Persian campaign against Greece via the Cyclades. The first destination for the Persian invasion fleet was Rhodes, where Lindos was besieged (apparently unsuccessfully); then the Persian commander

Datis led his force up the Ionian coastline to Samos before driving eastward through the Ikarian Sea to Naxos, which suffered severe destruction, including the burning of many of its temples. The island of Paros – a Persian ally – became the next stopping-off point before the campaign moved to the Greek mainland and intensified, with the Persian fleet anchoring in the bay at Karystos in Euboia. The Persian forces used Karystos as a base from which Eretria was taken in a major six-day operation. From here, the next Persian objective was Attica, and Marathon was selected as the ideal invasion point, located just to the north-east of Athens.

Persian Empire territory, 492 BC
Persian vassal state, 492 BC
Persian advance to Marathon Bay
Greek states at war with Persia
Neutral or medized states

The Opposing Sides

It must always be remembered when referring to the Greek 'army' or Persian 'army' in ancient times that these were not necessarily socially or even ethnically homogenous bodies. Classical Greece was not a nation state, but rather from the 8th century BC a collection of often geographically isolated city-states (*poleis*, singular *polis*), developing largely independently of one another although forming occasional leagues and alliances, typically to face a common threat. Thus rather than homogenize 'the Greeks', we instead speak of the soldiers of the individual city-states, although the system of the fighting hoplite was a pervasive one throughout the geographical territory of modern Greece, with regional variations. Similarly, when we talk of 'Persia' in this book we refer to the vast Near Eastern and Central Asian territory of the Achaemenid Empire, founded in 550 BC by Cyrus the Great (r. 559–530 BC). The empire had multiple administrative centres dotted throughout its territory and also one of history's first great standing armies, financed by the enormous wealth of the empire. At its height, the Persian standing army numbered some 150,000 soldiers, to which could be added thousands of men from literally dozens of client states within the empire. Even the elite core of the army – the 10,000 'Immortals' (so called because the formation was permanently kept at full strength) who formed the royal guard and a high-status body of infantry – included not only Persians but also other ethnic groups, such as Medes and Sacae. So when the Greeks and Persians went to war, the battles were fought not by unitary national armies, but by collections of individual state forces bound together in a common purpose.

TRAINING AND SERVICE

It can be quite difficult, from a modern perspective, to understand the way in which military service, or at least martial knowledge, in the ancient world

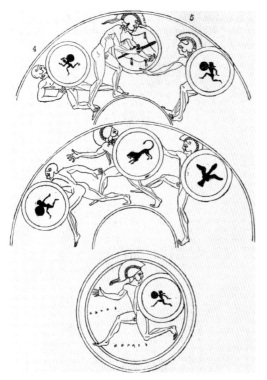

was deeply interwoven with notions of citizenship, masculinity and service. The Classical world, for all its intellectual urbanity, was a place of heightened and real threat, states and empires constantly engaged in either a political chess game with rivals or actively fighting for their own survival. Giving military service, therefore, or holding such service in readiness, was not a choice of career but rather a fundamental contribution to the survival and prosperity of one's people. In some ways the closest modern analogy would be the State of Israel, with its militarized citizenry connected to a deep sense of territorial survival.

Greek

It is commonly held that, in contrast to Persia, the Greeks did not maintain standing armies, but rather formed armies temporarily from an amateur citizenry, conscripted as required. This summary can produce an inaccurate sense of the military potential and composition of the Greek states, suggesting states basking in peace and only periodically adopting the mind-set and putting on the armour of war. In fact, the reality is rather more nuanced. The city-state of Sparta is an obvious exception (discussed in more detail below), in which virtually the whole of the Spartan male citizenry was in essence a standing army, constantly trained and exercised to readiness, and with no other profession but warrior. Even among many other of Greece's *c*.1000 *poleis*, however, elements of a standing force could be found at various times and periods, particularly during periods of tyranny. Navies and cavalries also needed maintaining in permanent readiness through budgetary investment, training and logistics. Furthermore, the primary sources do acknowledge small

ABOVE LEFT
Greek military training was largely an exercise in athletic competition, often conducted while carrying and wearing the essential kit of hoplite service. In this image from E. Norman Gardiner's *Greek Athletic Sports and Festivals*, we see hoplites engaged in a relay foot race in armour. (Internet Archive Book Images/Wikimedia/Public Domain)

ABOVE RIGHT
An Attic vase from the 5th century BC, showing the fight between two hoplite warriors. Clean, quickly fatal blows would have been a rarity in these actions; succumbing to blood loss from multiple smaller injuries would have been common, the lethal blow coming when the warrior no longer had the energy to offer an effective defence. (Christophel Fine Art/Universal Images Group/ Getty Images)

3

4

5

6

This Athenian warrior at Marathon shows the classic uniform and equipment of a hoplite of the 5th century BC. He is a member of the Aiantis (IX) tribal regiment, which held the right flank of the Greek battle line at Marathon, and is in his early twenties, having passed through his ephebic training between the ages of 18 and 20. His youth and vigour – imbued both by military training and agricultural labour – would usually mean that he occupied the frontal ranks of the hoplite phalanx, while the older members supported in the ranks further back.

Weapons, dress and equipment

The warrior would have paid for his own uniform and equipment. His principal weapon is the *dory* spear (**1**), held typically in an overhand grip at a leather grip section, with the spearhead presented forward and the multi-function *sauroter* counterweight tip to the rear. The back-up weapon was commonly the double-edged *xiphos* sword (**2**), secured in a leather or wooden scabbard from either a waist strap or, as shown here, a cross-shoulder strap.

The warrior has a Corinthian-style helmet (**3**) with its distinctive decorative horsehair plume; the helmet offered full head and face protection, but could be suffocating to wear in very hot weather. Protection for his torso comes from a composite cuirass (**4**), made principally from leather panels over bronze or iron plates, with exposed bronze scale armour on the flanks. The whole cuirass was structured around four hinged panels, with the shoulder sections tied in place at the centre of the chest. Lower leg protection came courtesy of two metal greaves (**5**), formed to the shape of the wearer's legs and held in place purely by the tension of the metal. In his left hand the hoplite carries an *aspis* shield (**6**), also later referred to as the *hoplon*, this one made from a thick body of wood with a thin bronze facing, decorated with individual, tribal or unit motifs. On the felt-lined interior we can see the bronze *porpax* armband (**7**) on his forearm, with his hand reaching through to grip the *antilabe* strap running around the rim. Viewed from the rear, it is apparent how much protection the *aspis* provided, shielding the soldier's body from the chin to the upper thigh.

standing forces in certain Greek *poleis* during the 5th and 4th centuries BC, in states such as Thebes, Argos, Syracuse and Elis, although these forces do seem more prolific in the 4th century BC than in the first half of the 5th century BC, probably in response to the perennial conflicts sweeping through the Classical lands. Regardless, the Archaic Greek city-states could still martial themselves for war effectively by drawing their citizens into service.

To ensure that these citizens were ready to fight, there had to be some process of militarization, forged through a relationship between social status and military service. Taking Athens as an example, during the 6th century BC, the *archon* (chief magistrate) Solon reformed the Athenian class system and its relationship to the city's political structure and armed forces. Four classes were defined. At the lowest level were the *thetes*, poor labourers or craftsmen who were used as light infantry (slingers, archers and javelin men) or as oarsmen in the Athenian navy, on account of their being unable to afford any more expensive weaponry and kit. (Note that in my presentation of the classes here I focus purely upon military responsibilities in relation to the class structure; there were also important links to participation in the political process that are not explained here.) Above the *thetes* were the *zeugitai*, largely semi-affluent farmers who had the means to purchase and maintain the kit of the hoplite warrior. (Their name, which translates as 'yoked men', basically referred to the way in which the hoplites were closely arrayed in the phalanx.) The next class tier up was occupied by the *Hippada Teluntes* ('horse breeders'), wealthy individuals of high social status who had the means to provide a horse and the associated equipment and support personnel to become a *hippias* (cavalryman), although if they so chose they could also serve in the hoplite ranks. Finally, at the top of the tree, were the *pentakosiomedimnoi* ('five-hundred-bushel men'). These men, being the very wealthiest of society, had sufficient status to be elected as one of Athens' ten *strategoi*, or generals. Note, however, that the members of the *pentakosiomedimnoi* could also serve as either cavalry or hoplites. Layered upon this sort of democratic feudalism was the organization of Greek male citizens into social 'tribes', social bodies organized by politico-military groupings rather than ancestral bloodlines (see page 78).

Although the warrior mentality, expressed particularly through hunting activities, would have surrounded the Athenian boy from his infancy, his journey into practical militarism began when he turned 18 years old and was sworn into service in the Temple of Aglauros, which stood on the Acropolis. His pledge provides a useful window into the mind-set of the citizen-soldier:

> I shall not dishonour these sacred arms, nor leave the man stationed beside me in the line. I will defend both the sacred and secular places and not hand over the fatherland smaller, but greater and mightier as far as I and all are able, and I shall listen to those in power at the time and the laws which have been drawn up and those that will be, and if anyone will abolish them I shall not give away to them as far as I and all are able, and I will honour the ancestral cults. My witnesses are the gods Aglauros, Hestia, Enyo, Enyalios, Ares and Athena Areia, Zeus, Thallo, Auxo, Hegemone, Herakles, the boundaries of the fatherland, and her wheat, barley, vines, olive and fig trees. (Quoted in Sekunda 2002: 5–6)

Once sworn in, the new recruit then embarked on two years of military training, known as the *ephabate*; the individual himself was an *ephebos*. The first year of training was devoted largely to giving the young man the physical attributes of a warrior. Socratic dialogues include references to how powers of bodily strength and endurance were not mere matters of self-improvement, like a modern gym membership, but were actually part of the citizen's obligations to his state and also to the soldiers who would stand next to him on the field of battle. The physical sculpting was mainly delivered through a series of athletic contests, focused upon running races, either individual or team relay events. These races might be run at public festival events as well as during private training. One particularly specialist event was the *hoplitodromos* (hoplite race), in which the young man, labouring under full hoplite gear, had to run a distance of two *stades* – about 350–400m – demonstrating brisk speed and focused endurance. Note that the distance involved in the race was actually a simulation of battlefield endurance and survival; in effect, the youth was training to run quickly through the shower of missiles, although in the reality of battle the final charge would have been conducted over a much shorter distance, to conserve energy. To give the new recruit a sense of how to handle weapons and conduct offensive and defensive movements, he might also practice the *Pyrrhichios*, or 'Pyrrhic dance'. In this exercise, the *ephebos* would perform sequences of quick, formulaic movements to represent the actions of fighting with sword, spear and shield, similar in a way to the *kata* performed by practitioners of karate today.

While the first year of Athenian hoplite training was largely focused on physical development, during the second year the emphasis shifted to more practical experience of military life. The young soldiers would undertake active military duties such as manning forts and watchtowers, conducting border patrols and training alongside veteran soldiers in garrisons, the barracks often located away from home. Once the young man had passed through his first two years of training, he was thereafter deemed as a hoplite until his late twenties, but stayed in a reserve status until the age of 50 or, in the case of Sparta, even until 60. (The nature of reserve status varied from state to state, but broadly followed the Athenian lines.)

This Attic black-figure lip cup shows a hunter about to launch a spear; a bull with a spear in its shoulder is shown just off this photograph. In Archaic and Classical Greece, hunting was classed as an activity that blended seamlessly with warrior skills. (Werner Forman/Universal Images Group/Getty Images)

Persian

The details of Persian military training have mainly come down to us via Xenophon, Strabo and Herodotus. Strabo's *Geographica* (7 BC), despite being written several hundred years after the principal events of this book, provides us with a sense of how the Persian youth was transformed from boy to warrior:

> From the age of five to twenty-four years they are taught to use the bow, to throw the javelin, to ride, and to speak the truth. They have the most virtuous preceptors, who interweave useful fables in their discourses, and rehearse, sometimes with sometimes without, music, the actions of the gods and of illustrious men. The youths are called to rise before day-break, at the sound of brazen instruments, and assemble in one spot, as if for arming themselves or for the chase. They are arranged in companies of fifty, to each of which one of the king's or a satrap's son is appointed as leader, who runs, followed at command by the others, an appointed distance of thirty or forty *stadia* [roughly 5.5–7.5km]. They require them to give an account of each lesson, when they practise loud speaking, and exercise the breath and lungs. They are taught to endure heat, cold, and rains; to cross torrents, and keep their armour and clothes dry; to pasture animals, to watch all night in the open air, and to eat wild fruits, as the terminthus, acorns, and wild pears. These persons are called *Cardaces*, who live upon plunder, for 'carda' means a manly and warlike spirit. The daily food after the exercise of the gymnasium is bread, a cake, cardamum, a piece of salt, and dressed meat either roasted or boiled, and their drink is water. Their mode of hunting is by throwing spears from horseback, or with the bow or the sling. In the evening they are employed in planting trees, cutting roots, fabricating armour, and making lines and nets. The youth do not eat the game, but carry it home. The king gives rewards for running, and to the victors in the other contests of the *pentathla* (or five games). The youths are adorned with gold, esteeming it for its fiery appearance. They do not ornament the dead with gold, nor apply fire to them, on account of its being an object of veneration. (Strabo XV.3.18)

In his *Cyropaedia*, Xenophon confirms the broad information given by Strabo, with some variations and embellishments. Xenophon notes that in addition to their instruction in hunting and martial skills, the young men would also be given duties guarding public buildings and other civic locations, to breed a sense of responsibility, self-discipline and public mindedness.

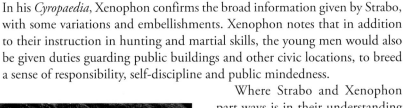

An ancient rock engraving of a hunter or mounted warrior, found in present-day Iran. The Persian horse-archers of the 5th century BC were immensely skilled to be able to fire on the run, especially as the invention of the saddle and stirrups was far in the future. (ATTA KENARE/AFP/Getty Images)

Where Strabo and Xenophon part ways is in their understanding of Persian military service following 'graduation' to the class that Strabo calls 'mature men'. For Xenophon, the warrior's full military service ran between the ages of 17 and 27, with a further 25 years remaining in a reserve status. Strabo, meanwhile, states that military training lasted until the man was 24 years old, but that 'They serve in the army and hold commands from twenty to fifty years of age, both as foot-

Enamelled tiles from Susa give a rare insight into the colours displayed by the Persian archers. Note the complete lack of armour; the Persians were largely an army oriented towards light infantry and cavalry. (The Print Collector/Print Collector/Getty Images)

soldiers and as horsemen' (Strabo XV.3.19). The implication is that the main period of service was given by men 20–24 years of age, but that the soldier remained on reserve status until he was 50. Strabo and Xenophon cannot be reconciled in the details, except perhaps by the passage of time between the two writers, but on the basic sequence of training, service, reserve status they are in agreement. Xenophon further clarifies the nature of life in the reserve:

> ... if they are needed in the interest of the commonwealth in any service that requires men who have already attained discretion and are still strong in body. But if it is necessary to make a military expedition anywhere, those who have been thus educated take the field, no longer with bow and arrows, nor yet with spears, but with what are termed 'weapons for close conflict' – a corselet about their breast, a round shield upon their left arm (such as Persians are represented with in art), and in their right hands a sabre or bill. (Xenophon, *Cyropaedia* I.2.13)

COMBAT Persian warrior

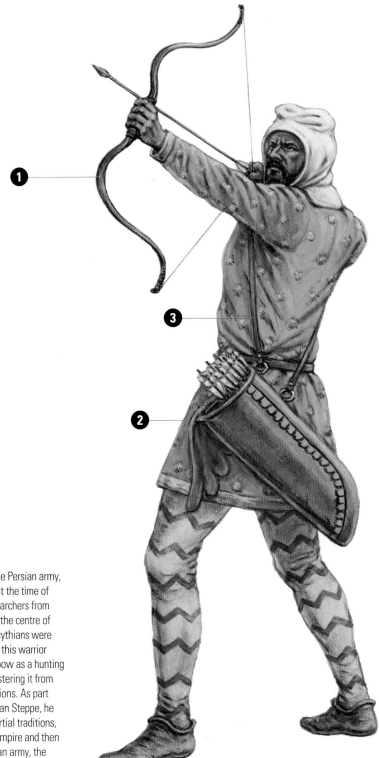

Archers formed an integral part of the Persian army, far more so than in the Greek army at the time of Marathon. Here we have one of the archers from the c.1,000 Scythians who occupied the centre of the Persian line at Marathon. The Scythians were known for their skills in archery, and this warrior would have been introduced to the bow as a hunting weapon in his early youth, likely mastering it from both mounted and dismounted positions. As part of a nomadic people from the Eurasian Steppe, he would also have been imbued in martial traditions, at first in opposition to the Persian Empire and then as its ally. As part of Darius I's Persian army, the warrior would have journeyed further west than he would have imagined possible in his youth.

Weapons, dress and equipment

The main weapon here is a composite recurve bow (**1**), here held at a high angle ready to deliver arcing fire down into the Greek ranks. The sizes, designs and profiles of Persian bows varied, from compact weapons such as this one, used to fire from horseback or in medium-range (up to *c.*100m) infantry encounters, to longer versions reaching out up to and beyond 150m. Whatever the shape or size, the recurve profile and the use of composite materials gave such bows terrific elasticity and power on release. Up to 75 arrows could be stored in the leather or hide *gorytos* quiver (**2**), typically suspended from a shoulder-strap system (**3**) on the left hip (for a right-handed shooter).

The archers' dress was, as far as the sources reveal, largely like that of other Persian light infantry, consisting of a loose-fitting thigh-length tunic (**4**), belted at the waist, leggings (**5**) and leather shoes (**6**), if the soldier did not fight barefoot. A white linen or coloured headdress (**7**) provided excellent protection from sunlight and heat – essential considering the Persian army's Middle Eastern and southern European area of operations – but no protection from enemy weapons. Although some Persians did wear armoured breastplates, it was common for soldiers to go into action without any armour at all. This left them vulnerable to spears and swords in close combat, but also gave them the advantages of speed and manoeuvrability on foot.

A useful insight in the reliefs at Persepolis, Iran: a Scythian archer led by a Median warrior. Both the Scythians and the Medes were warrior-like peoples, the former's nomadic lifestyle producing men who were extremely capable archers, both on horseback and on foot. (Photo by Roger Viollet/ Getty Images)

Xenophon's portrayal of the reserve soldiers has an honesty about it, in that Persian society seemed to recognize that after a decent interval away from military service, a former soldier's military skills were likely to have degraded significantly in using weaponry such as bows, which require constant practice and refreshed body mechanics to use well. Thus the reserve soldiers were purposed mainly as infantry mêlée troops, destined for blunt close-quarters combat that required more courage than talent.

KIT AND EQUIPMENT

All foot soldiers of the Archaic and Classical world were armed with roughly similar weapons and kit, with some variation due to the strata of wealth and society that the warrior occupied. The primary fighting tools of the Greek and Persian Wars of the 5th century BC were swords and stabbing spears for close-quarters fighting, and javelins, bows and slings as missile weapons, for delivering attrition up to ranges of several hundred metres, depending on the weapon construction and handling. For defensive protection, there were the obligatory shields, ranging from small lightweight varieties providing only partial torso protection, through to long two-handed battering shields that covered nearly the entire front of the torso and lower limbs, plus helmets and (if the warrior could afford it) personal body armour. While the essential tools were generically the same, however, there were some important differences in the detail between Greeks and Persians, partly in design and partly in distribution.

A 6th-century BC relief from the north frieze of the Siphnian Treasury in Delphi, Greece, showing the Battle of the Giants. The central hoplite figure, with rather confusing perspective, has drawn his *xiphos* sword for close-quarters fighting. (DEA/ARCHIVIO J. LANGE/De Agostini/Getty Images)

Greek

The Greek army of the 5th century BC was almost purely hoplite in composition. Two items of kit, above all else, defined the hoplite: his shield and his spear. The *dory* was a thrusting, not a throwing, spear, typically held during the fight with an overhand grip to thrust over the top and around the right side of the shield into the ranks of the enemy opposite. In construction the spear was typically 2–2.7m in length, the extension ensuring a good stand-off distance even in close-quarters combat. The shaft of the spear was ideally made from cornel or ash, two of the few woods that imparted the necessary flexibility to resist breaking, but also the rigidity to handle the impact of a strike. The shaft thickened slightly towards the rear of the spear and tapered towards the front, this placing the centre of gravity about a third of the way along the shaft, indicated by a leather grip section. Locating the centre of gravity here ensured that the majority of the spear's length was in front of the fighter, and that wielding the spear placed minimal strain on the arm muscles (total weight of the spear was around 0.9–1.8kg). The business-end of the spear was fitted with an iron leaf-shaped blade head, iron rather than bronze being used to avoid too much weight at the front. The broad shape of the spearhead, with its sharp point and double cutting edge, ensured a deep and wide penetrating wound. At the other end of the spear was a bronze *sauroter* counterweight, with a translation of 'lizard killer', showing that the ancient Greeks also had a sense of humour. Made from bronze, and therefore providing counterweight properties, the *sauroter* was principally used to stick the spear securely in the ground when it was not in use, the shaft resting against the warrior's shoulder. It has been claimed that the *sauroter* could also be used as a secondary spear tip should the main spear tip be broken in combat. We have no direct evidence of this, apart from the fact that in combat human beings will improvise at every level should their weapon be broken, and that the *sauroter* was perfectly capable of inflicting a nasty wound.

The spearhead and *sauroter* counterweight from Greek spears dating to the 6th century BC. Both of the pieces have socket fittings, which would have fitted tightly onto the spear haft, secured in place with pitch glue and sometimes nails. (DEA/G. DAGLI ORTI/De Agostini/Getty Images)

Complementing the spear was the *aspis* shield. The thin bronze covering sometimes (but not always) applied to the shields has led to a popular misconception that the *aspis* was made from metal. In fact, it was formed mainly from wood, typically poplar or willow – woods that deformed under impact rather than split (pine and lime would have been other options). The stressed bronze covering, if applied, went up and over the rim of the shield in a crease-free manner that still challenges modern-day metal workers. The interior of the shield was lined with coloured fabric, and in its centre was the bronze *porpax* armband that went around the left forearm near the elbow, the hand gripping the *antilabe* strap fitted just behind the 3 o'clock position on the right rim. A decorative cord ran around the inside rim.

The finished shield was a substantial affair, measuring about 0.8m in diameter and, depending on the construction and thickness of the wood used, could weigh anywhere from 3.5kg to 9kg. In terms of protective properties, the *aspis* shield would certainly have been able to stop sword cuts or spear jabs, although some authorities have claimed that it was less protective against powerful close-range arrow strikes.

In addition to a spear, the Greek hoplite would carry a sword, hung in a scabbard on his left hip from a cord that looped over his right shoulder. There were two main types of sword carried by the hoplite. The most common is generally referred as the *xiphos*, and was a single-handed weapon with a double edge, mostly with parallel sides but typically a leaf-shaped swelling towards the tip, giving it a diamond or lenticular cross-section and a sharp penetrating point. The *xiphos* sword could be used for both cutting and stabbing, and blade length was usually 50–60cm, although some examples drop as short as 30cm. Two less common types of hoplite sword were a single-edged recurved sabre, variously called a *kopis* or (by Xenophon) a *machaira*, and a falchion-like blade. Looking rather like a large *kukri* knife, the weight of the *kopis* leaned heavily towards the tip of the blade, hence it was used to deliver heavy cutting blows. The falchion, which to confuse matters seems also to be known as a *machaira*, also had a single-edge cutting blade, but with a straight or slightly concave back.

The spear, sword and shield were the main fighting tools of the Greek hoplite. In terms of his general fighting kit, he donned various types of personal armour. A composite form of cuirass consisted of articulated metal plates, covered in leather or linen and often featuring exposed sections of brass scale armour, particularly around the waist and on the upper torso.

Overlapping *pteruges* (scales, lit. 'feathers') provided an armoured skirt to protect the groin and upper thighs. Lighter forms of cuirass were made purely of thick sections of linen, leather or other fabrics, multiple layers of which were glued together with animal fat to form the *linothorax*, although the historical record of this armour is patchy and interpretative, and it might just have been a different take on the composite armour described above. More expensive items of body armour included the bronze 'muscle cuirass'; a metal chest protector literally contoured to reflect an ideal heroic musculature, pinned together around the torso in two sections. For the lower limbs, anatomically shaped bronze greaves could also be worn to protect the legs from the knees to the shins – parts of the body that were vulnerable to low sword or spear attacks.

One of the defining pieces of hoplite armour was the helmet, usually fitted with an elaborate and high horsehair crest on the top. One common type of helmet during our period was the Corinthian type, which provided full protection for the skull, cheeks, jaw and nose, albeit to the detriment of vision. There were several other types of helmet, however, with variation based on regional preferences. The Phrygian or Thracian helmet had a prominent forward-leaning curved apex atop the skullpiece, while the Chalcidian helmet was far plainer, with the cheek pieces either integral with the dome or fitted separately on hinges. Typically the warrior would wear a fabric headband or cap beneath the helmet, to give the helmet a better fit and a greater degree of comfort in the field.

Persian

The fact that the Persians, unlike the Greeks and later Romans, seem to have been broadly unconcerned with detailing their military means educated guesswork plays a role in describing their kit and equipment, the chief sources being the decorative arts. Compared to the Greek hoplites, the Persian warriors were far less armoured, largely preferring the advantages of mobility over the encumbrance (and expense) of heavy defensive gear. As Strabo indicates, the uniforms were extravagantly colourful, with yellows, purples and blues dominating, the colours and patterns indicating the unit to which the soldier belonged. In most of the visual depictions, the soldiers generally appear to be without any body armour or even helmets. The heavy infantry – the *sparabara* – would have been equipped with a long, rectangular wicker-and-hide shield large enough for a whole man to hide behind, and armed with a *c*.1.8m stabbing spear, significantly shorter than the Greek weapon. The archers who shared the protection of the *sparabara* shields, and also the Persian cavalry, were equipped with a variety of bows, the designs varying according to the regional style of the unit and the individual skills of the bowmaker. In many of the visual primary sources, the infantry are equipped with relatively short recurve composite bows. Unlike self-bows, which were made from a single piece of wood, the composite bows were constructed through a lamination of wood, horn and sinew, the sinew on the outer face of the bow to deliver greater elastic contraction on the release, while the horn was on the belly of the bow, storing up compression energy during the draw of the bow. These were powerful weapons, but they also required powerful men to operate them, the pull weight sometimes exceeding 50kg. Up to 75 arrows could be held in the *gorytos* quiver, although 50–65 were more likely.

One of the other bow types in evidence is the longer, straighter Elamite type, measuring up to 1.2m in strung length (the shorter varieties of Persian bows could be 0.9m long). These would have been used mainly to deliver

A reconstructed recurved sabre, a type of sword wielded by Greek and Persian alike, although straighter cut-and-thrust swords appear to be more common. The sword would be used in an angular chopping motion, favoured target areas being the neck and shoulders and the thighs. (DEA/C. BALOSSINI/De Agostini/Getty Images)

long-range fire from distances out to 150m and beyond. It has been claimed (see Fink 2014: 36) that the short Persian bows would have been used almost exclusively by the cavalry, who appreciated the compact weapon's dimensions when manoeuvring on horseback, while the longer bows were the choice of the Persian infantry. The visual primary sources, however, do not appear to present such a neat division. As noted above, infantry are often shown with short (sometimes very short) recurve bows, especially of the Scythian type with its 'double-S' profile. While the shorter bows would not have the reach of the longer types, they would have been far more convenient to use when the archers moved forward with infantry to ranges of 50m and below, these weapons being more practical for delivering direct fire amid jostling ranks.

The Persian cavalry, although they became increasingly armoured as the 5th century BC wore on, were during the first decades of the century largely equipped in the same manner as the infantry. Herodotus (VII.84) mentions that numbers of the Persian cavalry opted to wear helmets made of bronze and iron, these providing protection for the skull, cheeks and the nape of the neck. At the time of our battles, however, the most likely form of headgear would have been a simple soft cap. Cavalry weapons primarily consisted of a pair of throwing javelins, which could also be used for stabbing attacks, plus a short *kopis*-like sword. Battle-axes and bows were also used.

The descriptions of the Persian warriors above must always be balanced against the fact that the Persian campaign army during the 5th century BC could contain large numbers of foreign imperial troops – Lydians, Scythians, Parthians, Arians, Assyrians, Carians, Ethiopians and many others – each with their own patterns of dress and types of equipment. Therefore among the ranks of the Persian-allied forces there must have been numerous subtle variations in shields, spears, javelins, axes, clubs and battering weapons.

ABOVE LEFT
A regimented frieze at Persepolis depicts the Persian Immortals, armed with spears and bows. In some ways, the Persians had a more robust command-and-control structure than the Greeks, based on a decimal system of unit organization with a clear chain of command down through the leaders of each unit. A group of ten men, for example, was led from the front by a *dekarchs* while to the rear of the men was a *pascadathapatis*, who served as the deputy to the *dekarchs* while also himself acting as the commander of a five-man unit. (DEA/ARCHIVIO J. LANGE/De Agostini/ Getty Images)

ABOVE RIGHT
A Persian soldier with spear and quiver. The Persian spear was often shorter than the version used by the Greek hoplite, and was used as a short-range stabbing weapon, although it could be thrown *in extremis*. (DEA/ARCHIVIO J. LANGE/De Agostini/ Getty Images)

TACTICS

Greek

Hoplite tactics and formations have been the subject of intense, and often contentious, study since the 19th century. The process of evaluating the tactics is still ongoing, new theories emerging via the investigations of historians and also the practical activities of re-enactment groups, the latter pressure-testing new theories with their authentically recreated gear.

So what can we say with reasonable confidence about Greek hoplite warfare? The Greek hoplites were drawn up into a tight phalanx formation, a formation that seems to have developed around the end of the 8th century BC, tied closely to the emergence of the *aspis* shield and the political emergence of the *polis*. The phalanx was formed of men in close-arrayed ranks, often eight men deep by hundreds of metres in length, although terrain and commander's preference could occasionally alter the depth and length of the phalanx dramatically – during the battle of Delium in 424 BC, the Thebans on the Athenian right wing drew up in ranks 25 deep.

The key to the tactical effect of the phalanx was sheer mass. The lateral lines of warriors stood side by side, close enough for each shield – all of which were presented forward as a unified face – to provide protection for the neighbouring soldier's left side, as well as the shield carrier's torso. The deep files provided a physical and psychological forward momentum to the phalanx, the man standing just behind the man in front, pressing his shield against the warrior's back in the *othismos*, or push. It has been commonly held that the rear ranks compacted forward, literally to shove the front two ranks through the enemy like a rugby scrum. Such is open to question largely on issues of practicality; extreme pressure in contact with the enemy could have made it very hard for the front ranks to fight effectively, and could potentially even have resulted in crush suffocations. Yet the phalanx structure would certainly have ensured that the phalanx did not falter during the advance and engagement, the front ranks doing the immediate fighting while the men behind added momentum and also stepped forward into the gaps created by the fall of the wounded and the dead.

The first stage of a hoplite battle would be, on command of the general, to form the phalanx into line facing the enemy, each hoplite knowing his precise place in the ranks. They would stand in preparation, shields rested on their knees and spears upright. On command, they would raise their shields and spears (the latter still likely in an underhand grip) and begin walking forward, sometimes to the cadence of music. The advance could be over a considerable distance – the Syracusans marched up to 8km during one battle in the Sicilian Expedition (415–413 BC) – and except on the flattest and most uniform terrain often resulted in a considerable disordering of the ranks, to which fear, inexperience and the varying fitness levels of the soldiers contributed. The impression of totally unified and close-ordered ranks meeting the enemy was therefore an ideal rarely attained. The best of the regional armies at achieving an ordered advance was the incredibly well-drilled Spartans, who marched into action to rhythms dictated on a flute.

Whatever state it found itself in, the hoplite phalanx might unleash itself in a charge – the *epidrome* – when the distance between the Greeks and the enemy closed to under 200m. Note that the phalanx formations were typically unarticulated, as forward was the least complex line of attack and therefore ideally suited to men who spent more of their time farming than practising battlefield formations. Some formations did hone the skills of mass articulation, however; again, Sparta stands out as skilled in this regard, especially in the unified movement of the phalanx to make a flanking attack against a weakened enemy.

Once the hoplite phalanx actually pressed up against the enemy, then the fight devolved into a brutal mêlée. The front rank of the hoplites would hunker behind its shields, ramming the faces and edges of the shields into their opponents while either thrusting with the *dory* or, if the spear was lost or broken, slashing at him with a sword. It was a brutal, horrifying business, the main targets being the enemy's throat, arms, abdomen, groin and thighs. If the phalanx could keep the forward pressure applied, and if their courage didn't waver, they would often carry the day against enemies less comfortable with such a battle of blood and compression.

Although the Greeks would later adopt more of a combined-arms approach to warfare, especially during the Peloponnesian War (431–404 BC) and under the military conquests of Philip II (r. 359–336 BC) and Alexander III of Macedon (r. 336–323 BC), during the Greek and Persian Wars of the first half of the 5th century BC the hoplite phalanx was by far their main tool of decision. There were some other types of soldier on the battlefield, however. The Greeks had archers, slingers and javelin-throwers in limited numbers, the restriction on their proliferation mainly due to the sheer length of time and degree of practice required to produce a man competent with a sophisticated missile weapon. (The light-infantry element of Greek armies often used mercenaries for this role.) For this reason, the *psiloi* light infantry tended to have a rather free-playing tactical role, moving around the edges, front of and rear of the phalanx formations to deliver their fire where needed. They would often work ahead of the hoplite advance, softening up the enemy ranks in preparation for the moving bludgeon of the hoplite force.

Persian

The contrast between the Greek tactics and those of the Persians was, as far as we can tell given the scarcity of Persian sources, conspicuous. Imperial context explains much of this difference. While the Greek city-states were relatively small, culturally and militarily isolated entities, the Persians dominated a vast territory that embraced numerous different approaches to warfare, incorporated into the empire's huge standing army. The Persian theatre of war was also primarily the arid flatlands of the Near and Middle East, hence they were used to spaces that allowed a high degree of mobility. All of these influences coalesced into something approaching a 'Persian way of war'.

The Persian army expressed itself through true combined-arms tactics. The *sparabara* were the heavy-infantry mêlée troops, providing a shield wall from behind which archers would operate. In complete contrast to the Greeks, one heavy infantryman might be at the front of a file of nine archers, the complete ten-man group known as a *dathabam*. As suggested by this composition,

A relief of the Immortals, at Persepolis, Iran. Only ethnic Persians or Medians could be members of the Immortals. They were formed, according to Xenophon, by Cyrus the Great as a Persian elite, acting as a royal guard and also a professional standing army in the midst of a multinational force of variable standards. Because of their high quality, they tended to be used in the most hard-pressed parts of the line, or to perform critical missions to turn the tide of the battle. The battle of Thermopylae offers a prime example of their status as trusted warriors; rather than being wasted in grinding frontal assaults against the Spartans, the Immortals were sent on a deep flanking mission around the Spartan rear, this manoeuvre initiating the Spartan defeat. Although the Immortals might have had a cavalry element, they are primarily depicted as heavily armed infantry, each warrior being equipped with a bow and arrows, a spear, a shield and a short sword. This mix of both close-quarters and distance weapons would make the Immortals a versatile unit on the battlefield, capable of fighting against the best of the Greek hoplites. (Vivienne Sharp/Heritage Images/Getty Images)

A two-wheeled chariot depicted on a marble sarcophagus from the Royal Necropolis of Sidon, Lebanon, c.350 BC. The shift from the four- to the two-wheeled chariot during the Bronze Age increased the chariot's speed (by reducing its weight) and also tightened its turning circle, making it more manoeuvrable. Chariots were an integral feature of warfare from the end of the Bronze Age (c.1600–1100 BC) through to the present period of study, often carrying the most venerated and aristocratic of fighters. Two men typically fought from the back – a driver and an archer – trundling around the battlefield at a vertiginous speed of about 16km/h, firing arrows or ramming into enemy infantry ranks. Chariots excelled on the flat, arid plains of Mesopotamia and Egypt, but fared less well in the mountainous and wooded terrain characterizing much of Eastern Europe and the Balkans. The battles that Persia fought in Greece often did not offer the geographical conditions required for the effective application of chariot forces. The widening use of chariot-hunting javelineers, introduced by barbarian invaders during the period known as 'The Catastrophe' (c.1200–900 BC), plus the rise of mounted cavalry (horses had been first domesticated then militarized during the 2nd millennium BC), meant a decline in the status and power of the chariot, although more so among some powers than others. (De Agostini Picture Library/ Getty Images)

a primary tactic of the Persians was to shower the enemy with withering clouds of missiles, hopefully breaking up the attacking ranks with blurring attrition before they even reached the Persian shieldmen. Indeed, given the limited numbers and the poor weaponry (compared to the Greek hoplite) of the Persian heavy infantry, the chances of their resisting a phalanx push were limited if it couldn't be broken up before it reached them. The range of engagement varied according to many battlefield factors, but typically the Greek lines would be entering the 'beaten zone' of the archers from about 200m out. A centrepiece of Persian tactics appears to have been simply to wait until the enemy came into range and then let the arrows do the work.

Another Persian tactical distinction from the Greeks could be the application of cavalry, which during the time of Cyrus the Great constituted about 10 per cent of the army, but during the 5th century BC swelled to about 20 per cent. The cavalry, including charioteers, would perform the role of fast, mobile shock troops, seizing moments of opportunity and attacking the enemy's front and flanks with their lances, javelins and swords, or making circular fast passes and deep pursuits while employing their composite bows. Cavalry could be used tactically as a darting tool of attrition, as a rapid-reaction force to attack weak points opening up in the enemy ranks, or to intercept enemy logistics. One important tactical limitation of Persian cavalry, however, was that they rode in the pre-stirrup and pre-saddle era on unshod mounts, hence they had limited stability on the horse. This meant that the riders were best suited to fighting on flat and uniform terrain, not the joltingly mountainous and variable landscapes they found in Greece.

Although the Persian emphasis on mobility and medium-range firepower can appear compelling to modern eyes, with our focus on manoeuvre warfare, there were still some fault lines running through the Persian tactical system. For a start, there were the problems attendant upon the sheer scale and multi-ethnic composition of the Persian forces. The heterogeneous nature of Persian armies meant that there were significant issues with tactical coordination, and especially battlefield communications – not all units and formations spoke the same language, nor did they share the same training, weapons or even logistical systems. Efforts by the Persian leadership to enforce centralized command and control were never wholly effective, meaning that units and commanders might exercise their own unilateral decision-making on the battlefield, thus fragmenting lines of advance and the integrity of ranks. Adding to the problems was the fact that large parts of the Persian force were composed of soldiers who had been impressed into service by an unpopular imperial overlord. This often sapped military motivation, and made for weak parts in the lines. On several occasions Herodotus describes the Persian forces as being driven forward unwillingly by corporal punishment – 'When Xerxes had passed over to Europe, he viewed his army crossing under the lash' (Herodotus VII: 56), for example. Such a situation was in marked contrast to the Greeks, who had the ultimate motivation of fighting for their homeland.

Also, fielding a largely unarmoured force meant that individual Persian soldiers were horribly vulnerable during close-quarters fighting with the Greeks, who tended to wear substantial body protection. Although a shield could be used to protect the torso, the Persians' calves, thighs, throats and faces were all exposed to the cuts and thrusts of well-trained Greek hoplites; a spear thrust to the lower leg would instinctively cause the Persian soldier to drop his shield guard, opening him up to a potentially fatal attack to the abdomen or chest. Of course, the Persians hoped to keep the enemy at some distance through the extensive use of archers, who would keep firing even at ranges of just a few metres. The tactical utility of the archers was unquestionable – any hoplite careless with his shield guard, or under-armoured, would often find part of his body shot through with an arrow, as Persian archers could display astonishing accuracy and quick reactions to just such an opportunity. Yet at the same time, the archers would often find a disciplined hoplite shield wall endlessly frustrating, as the thick Greek shields soaked up numerous arrow strikes. The *c.*60 arrows held in the *gorytos* quiver could be expended with alarming rapidity; once they were out of arrows, the archers either retreated back to replenish their supplies from special arrow carts, or pages might bring more up to the front; but once the hoplites had closed to close-quarters fighting distance, the unarmoured archers (if they hadn't retreated by then) had to fall back on whatever hand-held weapons and skills they possessed.

Both the light and heavy Persian infantry also had problems engaging the hoplite phalanx, apart from the already stated lack of armour. Their shields, particularly the wicker varieties, were vulnerable to being penetrated by the heavy Greek spears. To make matters worse, Persian spears were physically shorter than the Greek types, meaning that the Persian infantry in the front ranks began taking casualties before they could inflict casualties on the Greeks by means of hand-held weapons. The classic sword used by the Persians – the *akenakes* short sword – was about 41cm in overall length, significantly shorter than the 60cm blade on the hoplite *xiphos*, or the *kopis*, which had a blade measuring up to 65cm.

Having noted the limitations of Persian forces, however, we should recognize that their tactical flexibility at many times could be a bonus against armies with fragmented discipline and wavering tenacity. The combination of infantry and cavalry, and shock and missile troops, could break up formations and create gaps that were quickly exploited by the fast-moving Persians, who traded armoured protection for speed.

Marathon

490 BC

BACKGROUND TO BATTLE

By the dawn of the 5th century BC, the Persian Empire was already a vast territory whose growing shadow crept towards the Greek homelands. Under Cyrus the Great (r. 559–530 BC), the empire had extended (in terms of modern-day territories) east to west from Turkey to Pakistan, north to south from Uzbekistan to the Arabian Sea. Asia Minor fell under Persian purview, and with only the Hellespont separating the Greek mainland from Persian ambition, some Greek cities, including Athens, entered into expedient alliances with Cyrus the Great. Persian imperial growth continued apace under Cambyses II (r. 530–522 BC) and Darius I (r. 522–486 BC), Thrace and much of modern-day Egypt and Libya coming under Persian rule. Greece was increasingly hemmed in by Persian ambition. Athens above all felt the squeeze in 505 BC, when Artaphernes, the Persian satrap at Sardis, threatened the Athenians with 'ruin' if they did not accept the former Athenian tyrant Hippias back into their fold. Hippias had been ejected from the *polis* in 511 BC by a Lacedaemonian invasion, and the Athenians bluntly rejected both the threat and Hippias. The awkward alliance between Athenians and Persians was over.

The trigger for the battle of Marathon, however, was really the Ionian Revolt of 499 BC. The small territory of Ionia, on the eastern edge of the Aegean Sea, was led into revolt by Aristagoras, the tyrant of Miletus, who also appealed to various major players on mainland Greece for their support in shrugging off the Persian overlords. Sparta refused, shying away from getting embroiled in a distant expeditionary campaign, but Athens and Eretria complied, sending 20 and five triremes of men respectively. For a time, the Ionian Revolt had the momentum of most revolutionary movements,

When the Persians confronted Greece in the 490s BC, they were at the peak of their imperial confidence. This relief depicts the victory of Darius I over the usurper magus Gaumata. During his reign, Darius I extended the Persian Empire as far east as the Indus Valley. (DEA/W. BUSS/De Agostini/Getty Images)

capturing and inadvertently destroying (through an accidental fire) the Persian administrative centre of Sardis. Caria joined the ranks of the defiant, although Athens withdrew its practical support for the action once the Ionians began to suffer defeats in the land campaign.

The Ionian Revolt was finally crushed at the battle of Lade in 494 BC, but Persian ire towards the Greeks had been well and truly kindled. A huge Persian invasion fleet now began to make its punitive way across the eastern Aegean Sea, conquering the islands of Chios, Lesbos and Tenedos in 493 BC and absorbing Macedonia in 492 BC. In 491 BC, Darius made explicit demands for obeisance to many of the Greek states – requesting the symbolic offerings of 'earth and water' – most of which complied, apart from Athens and Sparta, who sent a clear message simply by killing the Persian envoys.

Now Darius was truly set for war with the Athenians. Under the supreme command of Datis, a vast invasion fleet and force was built and assembled. The primary sources give varying data regarding the size and composition of this force, ranging from about 80,000 to more than half a million men. Logical unpacking of the evidence by historians has rationalized the figure to a maximum of about 120,000 troops, of whom about 25,000 men were actually fighting troops (see Sekunda 2002: 20–25). Most of the fighting force was composed of infantry, but the fleet included a separate contingent of Persian cavalry, likely commanded by one Artaphernes the Younger (the other Persian commander at Marathon) and numbering some 1,000–2,000 men and mounts.

The explicit purpose of the Persian expedition was to subjugate the troublesome Athenians and Eretrians. The Athenians faced a daunting struggle. Against a far larger, cavalry-enabled Persian force, the Athenians

could present a purely hoplite force of citizen warriors and combatant slaves numbering about 9,000 men all told. To this strength was added the contribution of the Plataeans of Boeotia, likely to be about 1,000 men.

Leadership of the Athenian force fell to three main figures. The first, Callimachus of Aphidia, held the politico-military position of *polemarch*, essentially a form of commander-in-chief able to exercise authority over the ten *strategoi*. The leading *strategoi* on the day of the battle of Marathon – according to Herodotus, on campaign the command rotated through the ten *strategoi* on a daily basis – fell to one Miltiades, ageing scion of a family heavily associated with the politics of tyranny (Miltiades himself had been tyrant of the Thracian Chersonese). One of the advantages Miltiades brought was a familiarity with the Persian way of war, having been involved in Persian military expeditions during his time as a Persian vassal. Leading the Plataeans was Arimnestos, of whom we know little except that he was a long-standing (and therefore likely to be competent) military commander.

The Athenians and Plataeans were faced with an enemy at least double their number and with the advantage of momentum behind them. Following their suppression of the Ionian Revolt, the Persians had advanced across the Cyclades, taking Samos, Naxos and Paros before arriving at Euboia and anchoring in the bay of Karystos. Now the Persians enacted their revenge on the Eretrians; after a six-day campaign, Eretria was defeated and sacked.

Now the focus was on Athens. For the invasion of Attica, the bay of Marathon was selected as the Persian beachhead, possibly (according to Herodotus) on the advice of Hippias. Marathon was just 40km from Athens, and it offered several key advantages to the Persians, not least a broad, flat area in which to disembark and encamp their force plus, crucially, watering for the horses and men at Lake Stomi, at the western edge of the bay.

Having received news of the landing, the Athenians now wrestled with a hard tactical decision: wait for the Persians to advance out of Marathon and meet them near Athens itself, with all the logistical and psychological comfort that provided, or march out straight away and confront the Persians at Marathon. Arguing for the latter policy, Miltiades swayed the assembly, and so in August/September 490 BC, the Athenian hoplites, clad for battle, stepped out of the city to face an apparently unequal battle.

In this frieze from Athens, created around the time of the battle of Marathon, we see hoplites moving forward behind a horse-drawn chariot or wagon. The hoplites are carrying their spears in a non-combative manner, with the *sauroter* counterweight and spear rest pointing downward, the broad spear tip harmlessly up in the air. (DEA/G. NIMATALLAH/De Agostini/Getty Images)

MAP KEY

1 The Greek forces advance out from their camp to face the Persians on the Marathon plain. Both sides draw up their infantry units in lines of similar overall length, but the Greek centre is less deep than the usual hoplite formation to allow the line to extend further to match that of the enemy.

2 The Greek hoplite forces begin their attack, pressing forward against the Persian infantry. The Greek left and right flanks make steady progress against the Persians, but the less deep Greek centre begins to collapse under the unequal Persian pressure, and is eventually forced backwards.

3 The Greek centre retreats out of the hoplite line, allowing the Persian centre to push through. The retreating Greeks pull back towards their camp area around the Herakleion Shrine.

4 The Persian advance in the centre actually allows the Greek left and right flanks to turn inwards and make flanking

and rear attacks against the enemy penetration. At the same time, the force of the hoplite advance on the flanks overcomes Persian resistance, and the Persian troops fall back.

5 The routed Persians drop back into the Great Marsh, where many are hunted down and killed, or flee along Schoinias Beach in an attempt to board the offshore vessels and escape the massacre.

6 As the Persian flanks disintegrate, the Persian centre is effectively encircled and destroyed, cut off from the escape routes to the east.

7 Many Persians are killed on Schoinias Beach, even as they attempt to board their vessels. The Greeks, however, manage to destroy only a handful of Persian triremes, and the fleet escapes with its surviving forces and heads for Phaleron Bay, in an unsuccessful attempt to attack Athens while the city's soldiery is absent.

Battlefield environment

The bay of Marathon arced for roughly 7km in the far west of Attica. The Persian fleet anchored to the east of the bay in front of Schoinias Beach, a strip of sand about 3km long and sheltered to the east by the Kynosoura promontory. Inland from the eastern edge of Schoinias Beach was Lake Stomi, salty near its outflow into the sea, but offering fresh water for horses and men further inland. The Marathon plain was a flat expanse bordered by mountains to the west and north. Its topography was quite different from that of the plain today, which has been substantially drained. Dominating the land above Schoinias Beach was the extensive Great Marsh, essentially cutting off the east of the plain for military use. In the west was the

smaller Vreziza Marsh, south of what was then Marathon village. Just west of the village was the Herakleion Shrine, amid the olive trees of a sacred grove. Between the two marshes and the surrounding mountains, the rest of the plain consisted of land cultivated for cereal crops and pasture for livestock. The western half of the plain was bisected by the Athens–Oinoe road, on a north–south axis, and the road branched off towards Rhamnous to the north of the Great Marsh. The Charadros River possibly flowed down from the mountains into the centre of the battlefield. So while Marathon presented the Persians with a flat landing site, marshes, groves, rivers and mountains also constrained the possibilities of movement.

The Marathon plain as it is today, viewed from the Tomb of the Athenians; most of the Greek fallen were buried on the battlefield. (Tomisti/Wikimedia/CC BY-SA 4.0)

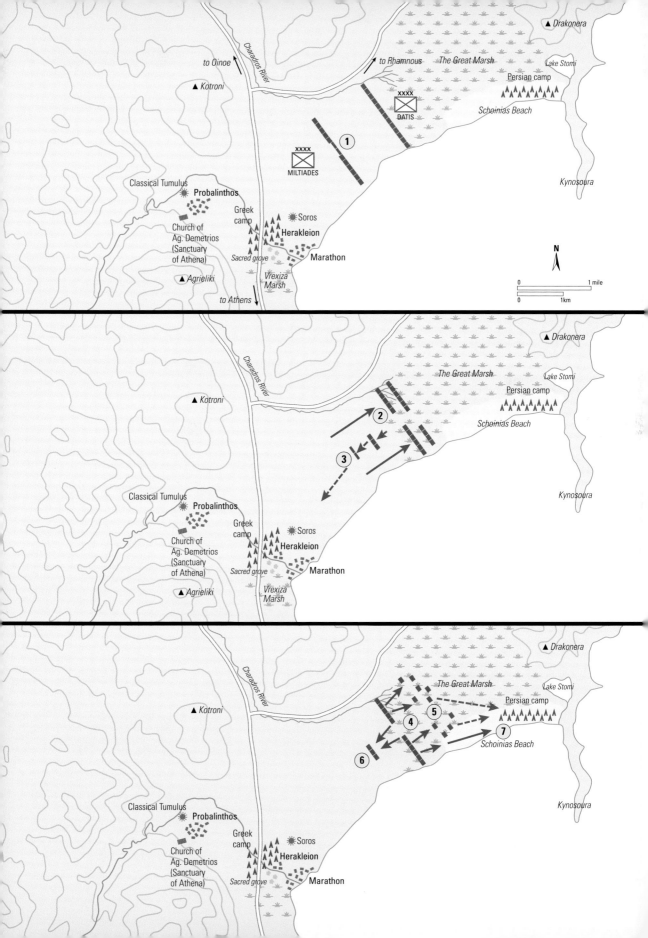

INTO COMBAT

By best estimates the Athenian force marched to Marathon on or around 3 September 490 BC. On their arrival, they camped on the west of the plain using the defensive protection afforded by their terrain – although the sources give room for interpretation, the likeliest option is that the Athenians had the Agrieliki Mountain on their left flank, with their right flank on the shoreline, making a confined front that prevented the Persians from utilizing their cavalry in flanking attacks. The Herakleion Shrine formed the heart of the Greek camp. Datis, meanwhile, appears to have adjusted his forces, possibly embarking half of his army, including all of his cavalry, most likely with the intention of sending a force to Phaleron Bay to conduct a direct assault on Athens, while the Athenian army was preoccupied at Marathon. This would prove to be a fatal error.

Once the Athenian and Plataean force arrived at Marathon, battle was not immediately joined; indeed the two sides faced one another for five or six days before the clash itself on or around 11 September. Why the wait? On the day the Athenians marched for Marathon, Athenian envoys made the journey to Sparta, to request Sparta's critical assistance at Marathon. The Spartans complied, but explained that there would be a delay in deploying on the campaign, for religious and practical military reasons (the *Karneios* festival and war with the Messenians respectively). The delay meant, in practical terms, that the Athenians would have to fight alone.

The other reason for the delay was that the Athenian *strategoi* were enmeshed in a debate about when to fight, or whether to fight at all. The ten *strategoi* were evenly divided in their opinion on the matter. On the one side were those who felt that the Athenians should avoid battle, given the towering scale of their adversary. The others, led by the tactically aggressive Miltiades, advocated an immediate attack against an enemy who, frankly, would not be expecting one. Herodotus explains how the impatient Miltiades summoned his powers of oratory to win the deciding vote of Callimachus:

> 'Callimachus, it is now in your hands to enslave Athens or make her free, and thereby leave behind for all posterity a memorial such as not even Harmodius and Aristogeiton left. Now the Athenians have come to their greatest danger since they first came into being, and, if we surrender, it is clear what we will suffer when handed over to Hippias. But if the city prevails, it will take first place among Hellenic cities. I will tell you how this can happen, and how the deciding voice on these matters has devolved upon you. The ten generals are of divided opinion, some urging to attack, others urging not to. If we do not attack now, I expect that great strife will fall upon and shake the spirit of the Athenians, leading them to medize. But if we attack now, before anything unsound corrupts the Athenians, we can win the battle, if the gods are fair. All this concerns and depends on you in this way: if you vote with me, your country will be free and your city the first in Hellas. But if you side with those eager to avoid battle, you will have the opposite to all the good things I enumerated.'

By saying this Miltiades won over Callimachus. The polemarch's vote was counted in, and the decision to attack was resolved upon. Thereafter the generals who had voted to fight turned the presidency over to Miltiades as each one's day

came in turn. He accepted the office but did not make an attack until it was his own day to preside. (Herodotus VI.109–10)

It is noteworthy that Miltiades managed to achieve his objectives on the day that he took over the role of commanding *strategos*; thereafter his name would forever by stamped with the victory at Marathon.

On the morning of 11 September, the Persians assembled themselves for battle, a wall of infantry some 1,400 men to the front and ten men deep, with thousands of archers nervously hooking the strings of their bows. The primary unit of the Persian forces was the *hazarabam*, the numerically descriptive 'thousands', each of 1,000 men. Ten of these units made a *baivarabam* ('10,000'). The centre of the force, where Datis himself stood, contained the elite of the army, a regiment of *arstibara* (the emperor's personal guard) and a *hazarabam* of 'Sacae', the Persian blanket term for Scythians. The cavalry were absent offshore, despite the ideal terrain.

Responding quickly to the Persian assembly, the Greek hoplites, fully regaled in their *panoply*, also formed up in their phalanx on the Marathon plain. Archaic Greek forces of the 5th century BC were composed of 'tribal' regiments (see page 78 for more details), each named after a Greek hero as follows: Aiantis, Aigeis, Acamantis, Antiochis, Erechtheis, Hippothontis, Kekropis, Leontis, Oineis, Pandionis. The exact placement of these regiments in the line of battle is not certain, apart from a few specific insights from Plutarch and Herodotus. What is important, however, is Herodotus' comment that 'As the Athenians were marshalled at Marathon, it happened that their

This painting by French artist Georges Antoine Rochegrosse (1859–1938) conveys a vivid picture of Athenian and Plataean warriors surging forward against the Persians at the battle of Marathon. It is probably accurate in showing the eventual loosening of the Greek phalanx in the charge. (Hulton Archive/Hulton Fine Art Collection/Getty Images)

line of battle was as long as the line of the Medes. The center, where the line was weakest, was only a few ranks deep, but each wing was strong in numbers' (VI.111). This detail is critical to the battle. By thinning out the centre of the line, possibly to just four ranks deep instead of eight, the Greeks would have been able to match the frontage of the Persians, albeit at the cost of an imperilled centre. At least the up-to-strength wings would guard against flanking attacks.

The two forces faced each other as the sun climbed higher into the morning sky, the sea forming the boundary for the Greek right and Persian left flanks. At this point they were some 1,500m apart. Then the Greeks began their advance, moving forward at a steady walking pace, closing down the distance while attempting to maintain the integrity of the ranks.

Possibly at around 200m, the hell of battle was unleashed. The Greeks broke into a run with a roar of voice, even as a hazy cloud of Persian arrows began to descend in a lethal hail, delivered to regular cadences, the Persian archers using the three-fingered pull technique (arrow nock lightly resting between the index finger and middle finger, but using all three top fingers to draw the string) to give maximum draw on their powerful bows. The hoplites angled their shields upwards, protecting the face and torso from many of the strikes. As they approached the Persian lines, the hoplites would have readied their spears, switching to an overhand grip. The Persians, sensing the coming impact, readied their stabbing spears and swords, and hunkered down behind their wicker shields.

The mêlée that followed the physical clash between the Greek hoplites and the Persian infantry can only be imagined in its horror. Shield met shield, each side applying forward pressure while stabbing at faces, arms, groins and

A battle of Marathon re-enactment shows the colourful Persian archers in action. The archers would have begun delivering their lethal hail of arrows at a range of about 200m, although they could reach further if need be. (LOUISA GOULIAMAKI/AFP/Getty Images)

legs with their spears. Persian *sparabara* leaned into their hide shields in an attempt to resist the Greek pressure, while Persian archers still fired arrows through the shield gaps at point-blank range into their frenzied opponents. In reality, only the first two ranks of the Greek hoplites were fully engaged, those behind applying forward pressure in the *othismos*. If spears were lost or broken, swords were drawn and the hacking battle began, the soldiers' adrenaline battling against the progressive exhaustion of muscle. This close-quarters attrition, according to Herodotus, continued for some length of time, but the battle was beginning to move towards a conclusion. As was to be expected, the Athenian line began to weaken in its thinner centre – held by the Leontis and Antiochis regiments – against the elite Persian core. Plutarch and Herodotus diverge in their accounts of the unfolding of this wrestle in the centre of the battlefield. Plutarch states that: 'In the battle, the Athenian center was the hardest pressed, and it was there that the Barbarians held their ground the longest, over against the tribes Leontis and Antiochis' (II.5.3), implying that the Persians in the centre did not relinquish their ground, at least at first. Herodotus, on the other hand, sees the Persian centre making more evident progress: 'The foreigners prevailed there and broke through in pursuit inland' (VI.113). For historians, Herodotus tends to prevail in the decorous struggle between primary sources. (Herodotus is largely considered by modern scholars to be one of the more reliable primary sources for this period, as many of his statements have been corroborated by research. Parts of his writing, however, are subject to bias, scientific inaccuracy or geographical misunderstanding, all of which admittedly affected most ancient writers to varying degrees.) Indeed, it is a popular notion that the Greeks actually deliberately weakened their centre to permit a breakthrough, in an act of tactical cunning. For while the Greek centre either ground to a halt or went into the retreat, the Athenian and Plataean wings pressed onwards with unrelenting strength, sufficient that the corresponding Persian wings began to stagger backwards and inwards. It was the beginning of the Persian collapse.

For the historian, it is tempting to polish the battle of Marathon into an image of tactical cleanliness, the Greeks giving way in the centre to allow their

flanks to hinge inwards and trap the Persians. In reality, the battle evolved with less deference to cartography and decision. We must remember that the hoplite force was unarticulated in nature, hence would have been unable to make unified turns over what was a very long battlefront. This fact also calls into question the belief that the Athenians deliberately withdrew in the centre to allow for the flanking surges. Hacking violence and the brute momentum of the hoplite phalanx at full depth are far more persuasive explanations for the success on the Greek wings. Herodotus explains that 'In victory they let the routed foreigners flee, and brought the wings together to fight those who had broken through the center' (VI.113), and this is the passage that has most fuelled the idea of a conscious Greek pincer action. Given the limits of Greek command and control and manoeuvrability, however, a more natural explanation would be that simply advancing on the flanks presented the Greeks with targets of opportunity to the centre, hence the direction of the attack would have moved both forwards and inwards.

Now chaos prevailed among the Persian ranks, as jolted retreat turned into panicked rout. Many of the Persian troops simply scattered, some being killed on the run, others drowning or being hunted down and slaughtered in the Great Marsh. Thousands attempted the most favourable option – escape back to their ships anchored on the shoreline on Schoinias Beach. The phalanx combat now dissolved into individual and small-group hand-to-hand actions on the beach. That the Persians still had some fight in them is attested to by the fact that the Athenians were only able to capture seven of the Persian ships; the rest managed to take aboard survivors from the on-land battle, then put to sea with a new urgent purpose – attack Athens directly with the remainder of the Persian army by landing in the city's main harbour at Phaleron Bay, while Athens was stripped of its fighting men.

Thus it was that the Greek victors at Marathon had little time to cast off their arms and bask in the sun and their victory. Instead they immediately embarked on a forced march of about 40km, reaching Athens in several hours and, crucially, ahead of the Persian fleet. The Persians anchored off the bay for a few days, but seeing that the Athenians were there in full force, and indeed were reinforced by 2,000 late-coming Spartans, they decided to trust to caution, and sailed back to Persia.

A group of modern re-enactors gather to present the battle of Marathon. The size of the shield in relation to its owner gives a good indication why hoplites were classed as 'heavy' infantry; the *aspis* would have been a substantial piece of equipment, not suited to quick manoeuvres. (LOUISA GOULIAMAKI/AFP/Getty Images)

The most pervasive legacy of the battle of Marathon has, of course, been the Marathon running race. The origins of the race are said to lie in the epic run of the Greek messenger Pheidippides, who sprinted non-stop to Athens following the victory at Marathon, bursting into the assembly to announce *Nenikēkamen!* ('We have won!'), before promptly dying as a consequence of his efforts. Back in 490 BC, however, the victory at Marathon must have electrified the populace with self-belief and obeisance to the gods. Given the tendency for ancient sources to get carried away with statistics, Herodotus' final casualty data seem imbalanced but reflect the magnitude of the Greek victory: 192 Greek dead against 6,400 Persians. If anything, Marathon appeared to be proof of the superiority of the hoplite way of war.

Thermopylae

480 BC

BACKGROUND TO BATTLE

The defeat at Marathon was undoubtedly a smarting blow for Persia, imbued as it was with a sense of imperial might and destiny. Persian humiliation would soon, however, crystallize into a fiery need for revenge. Indeed, what we today term the Greek and Persian Wars would continue with varying levels of intensity until 449 BC, roughly half a century of bloodshed as Persia sought to make Greece firmly bend the knee and offer the gifts of 'earth and water' that denoted subjugation.

It would take a decade after Marathon, however, for the Persians to return to Attica. Darius I died in 486 BC, and was succeeded by his son, the mighty Xerxes I (r. 486–465 BC), a cultured and intelligent individual, albeit with a personality distorted by being leader of the greatest empire ever seen. In 480 BC, having created a vast invasion fleet and trained his army at Sardis in 481 BC, Xerxes began what appeared to be an irresistible campaign against the Greek mainland. There appears to be little of sophistication in the overall campaign objectives, other than to absorb Greece finally into the Persian domain.

Herodotus gives a detailed account of the Persian army assembled for the invasion:

> The Greeks of Thrace and the islands off Thrace furnished one hundred and twenty ships, and the companies of these ships must then have consisted of twenty-four thousand men. As regards the land army supplied by all the nations – Thracians, Paeonians, Eordi, Bottiaei, Chalcidians, Brygi, Pierians, Macedonians, Perrhaebi, Enienes, Dolopes, Magnesians, Achaeans, dwellers on the coast of Thrace – of all these I suppose the number to have been three hundred thousand. When these

numbers are added to the numbers from Asia, the sum total of fighting men is two million, six hundred and forty-one thousand, six hundred and ten. This then is the number of soldiers. As for the service-train which followed them and the crews of the light corn-bearing vessels and all the other vessels besides which came by sea with the force, these I believe to have been not fewer but more than the fighting men. Suppose, however, that they were equal in number, neither more nor fewer. If they were equal to the fighting contingent, they made up as many tens of thousands as the others. The number, then, of those whom Xerxes son of Darius led as far as the Sepiad headland and Thermopylae was five million, two hundred and eighty-three thousand, two hundred and twenty. (Herodotus VII.185–86)

The figures given here run away into the realms of fancy – most historians place the Persian army at a strength of about 80,000 men all told – but Herodotus' account is useful for illustrating the sheer ethnic diversity of Xerxes' force, plus something of the logistics involved with transporting and supplying this massive army, grinding its way around the edge of the Aegean Sea.

Setting out from Sardis in April 480 BC, the Persian invasion army worked its way up through Asia Minor, crossed the Hellespont in early June (using vast floating bridges), advanced through Thrace and Macedonia, and by mid-August was bearing down through Thessaly, with Athens clearly in its sights. The Greek response by this stage was far from unified. The 'Hellenic League', dominated by Sparta and Athens, consisted of a collection of Greek states and islands, but it did not constitute the entirety of the Greek mainland by any means. Furthermore, Xerxes had been skilfully attempting to isolate Sparta and Athens through diplomatic enticements, or threats, to surrounding states. Once the might of the Persian invasion force became apparent, some league members defected to the Persians through outright fear, Thessaly being an important example.

Although Sparta's relationship with Athens had blown hot and cold over the previous decades, the Spartan king Leonidas I (r. 489–480 BC) had no desire to see Persian imperialism flood like oil around the Spartan state. Unlike at the battle of Marathon, Sparta would be at the forefront of the battle of Thermopylae.

The challenge for the Greek defence was to find the right place at which to meet and stop the Persians; a location that would, to some degree, annul the Persian advantage in numbers. That place was Thermopylae, located on a narrow coastal path overlooking the Malian Gulf, bordered on one side by the Kallidromos Mountains and on the other by the cliffs leading down to the waters of the Malian Gulf. At three points in particular – known as the West Gate, Middle Gate and East Gate – the pass was particularly narrow, measured in single metres. It was at the Middle Gate, just *c.*15m wide at the 'Phocian Wall' defences built by the Phikians against Thessaly, that Leonidas chose to make his stand.

Religious festivals, practicalities and the shifting nature of the Greek response meant that the Greek force at Thermopylae would be truly dwarfed by the approaching Persian army, which was perfectly aware of, and perfectly untroubled by, the Greek defence awaiting them. Herodotus explains the composition:

The Hellenes who awaited the Persians in that place were these: three hundred Spartan armed men; one thousand from Tegea and Mantinea, half from each place; one hundred and twenty from Orchomenus in Arcadia and one thousand from the rest of Arcadia; that many Arcadians, four hundred from Corinth, two hundred from Phlius, and eighty Mycenaeans. These were the Peloponnesians present; from Boeotia there were seven hundred Thespians and four hundred Thebans. In addition, the Opuntian Locrians in full force and one thousand Phocians came at the summons. (Herodotus VII.202–03)

A Greek hoplite and Persian warrior in battle, 5th century BC. This image shows with rare clarity the difference between Persian and Greek dress, and gives a good sense of the chopping action that was central to use of the curved sabre. (Coupe attribuée au Peintre de Triptolème/Wikimedia/Public Domain)

While doubtless appreciating the contribution of allies, Leonidas would have been perfectly aware that most of their forces were comprised of part-time citizen-soldiers, rather than well-honed warriors such as the Spartans. He therefore positioned them judiciously. The Phocians, with their local knowledge, he sent out into the surrounding mountains to guard possible routes from flanking attacks, especially the so-called Anopaia Path. The others took up positions alongside the Spartans at the Middle Gate, but it was clear that the small Spartan army – actually just Leonidas' royal bodyguard – was going to be the core of the defence.

MAP KEY

1 Day 1: The Persians conduct a major frontal assault on the Greek position around the Phocian Wall, repeatedly attacking the Greek lines with infantry and archery fire.

2 Day 1: The Spartans and their allies repulse the enemy onslaughts; throughout the day they make several forays forward into the Persian lines, each time pulling back to the defensive safety of the Phocian Wall.

3 Day 1: An attack by the famed and feared Persian Immortals is also blunted by the Spartans and Greeks. The Immortals subsequently move back to the west.

4 Day 2: More attacks by the Persian main force are stopped by the obdurate Greeks. Yet during the evening, the Immortals – led by the treacherous Ephialtes – begin their movement along the Anopaia Path, in an attempt to encircle the Greek defence.

5 Day 3: The Phocians posted as a rearguard for the Spartans come under a surprise attack from the Immortals on the Anopaia Path. Being a relatively small group, the Phocians are unable to stop the Immortals, and are driven away and isolated, the Immortals simply bypassing them and continuing onwards.

6 Day 3: The Immortals continue down the Anopaia Path unopposed to Alpenoi on the coast of the Malian Gulf. This brings them behind the Greek lines around the Phocian Wall – the Spartans are falling into a pincer trap.

7 Day 3: Having been alerted to the impending Greek encirclement, Leonidas allows most of the Greek force to escape to the east, leaving behind the Spartans, 700 Thespians and 400 Thebans.

8 Day 3: The Spartans pull back to the hillock of Kolonos, under the force of a major Persian assault from the west. There, trapped between a two-pronged Persian attack (the Immortals having moved up from the east), Leonidas' Spartans and most of the Greek allies are destroyed.

Battlefield environment

The Thermopylae Pass provided Leonidas with a superb defensive environment. The name 'Thermopylae' was etymologically related to the hot thermal springs in the region, but geographically referred to the 6.5km defile that ran between a mountainous interior, dominated principally by Mount Kallidromos (elevation 1,399m), and the waters of the Malian Gulf. The mountains were heavily covered by oak-tree growth and had a complex terrain that meant local knowledge was essential to travel through them without becoming lost and disoriented. The defile itself was extremely narrow in parts, squeezing to little more than 10m in places. At the Middle Gate, where Leonidas chose to make his stand, the pass was less than 100m wide, narrowing to about 15m wide by the large masonry blocks at the Phocian Gate. Above this towered 1,000m of precipitous mountain face, while on the coastal side steep cliffs fell away into the sea, making direct flanking attacks impossible. The weather in high summer would have been hot and bright, with temperatures reaching a seasonal average of around 27°C, with low humidity, even on the coast. The coastal paths would have been much as they are today – dusty and rocky – and the levels of physical discomfort in the ancient martial clothing and helmets must have been high.

A view of the Thermopylae Pass in the area where the Phocian Wall would have been located. Time has changed the pass considerably; when the battle was fought the coastline actually lay roughly along the line of the modern road. (Fkerasar/Wikimedia/ CC BY-SA 3.0)

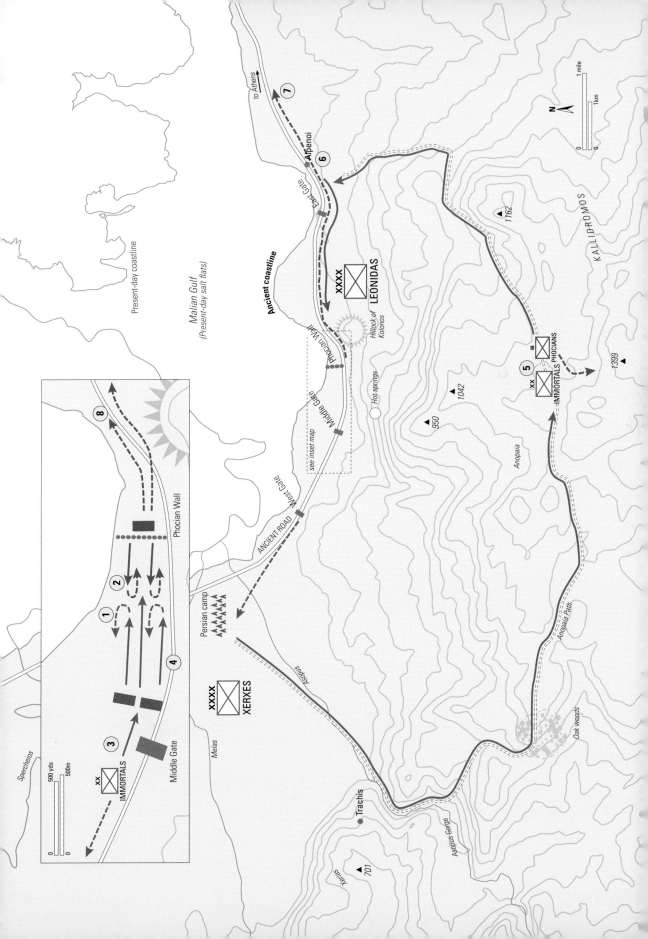

INTO COMBAT

Like Marathon, the battle of Thermopylae began with a pause. Xerxes arrived, confident at the head of his immense army, in August or September 480 BC and thereupon waited for four days in the Persian camp around the West Gate. According to Herodotus, the wait was simply due to the expectation that the Greeks would be intimidated by the Persian might and majesty into abandoning their positions without a fight. Envoys were sent to request the Spartan surrender, but were turned away without consideration.

On the fifth day of waiting, after what amounted to four days of rising disrespect towards Xerxes, the Persian king decided enough was enough, and launched his attack. The first troops he sent into action were a large group of Medes and Cissians. Median skills with the bow imply that the Spartans and their allies were treated with the customary hails of Persian arrows, fired from about 100m distance, although this lethal rain would have had less effect than intended under the cover of shields and the Phocian Wall. Having failed to resolve the issue through the use of missiles, the Persian troops then advanced into close-quarters action.

Here the brilliance behind the Spartan choice of defensive position became apparent. Although details of the battle are partial, it appears that a relatively small number of Spartans set themselves into the narrow passageway of the Phocian Wall, forcing the larger number of Persians to fight on an equal front. With shields locked, the Spartans formed a near-unbreachable phalanx, from which they were able to use their longer spears to great effect. Moreover, according to some sources, the Spartans also forayed out as if on the attack against the Persian camp, then turned in feigned retreat to draw on a Persian chase, introducing disorder into the enemy ranks. At the right moment, they then turned and fought again, utilizing their strengths in close-quarters fighting to inflict unexpectedly heavy casualties on the now shocked Persians.

Xerxes, alarmed at the lack of progress (Herodotus mentions that three times the king leapt from his throne as he observed the destruction of his units), eventually decided to send in his most trusted men, the Immortals. Their reputation was not enough to make headway against the Spartans either, and they were repelled with bloody effect.

The sun set on the first day, with the Greeks still in place and Xerxes unnerved by the disciplined foe. As Herodotus notes: 'The king was at a loss as to how to deal with the present difficulty' (VII.213). The fighting continued on the second day, but essentially with the same intractable results for the Persians. Details of the action on this day are particularly scarce, but Herodotus mentions that Leonidas rotated the city-state units through the front line, allowing recovery time for the Spartans and others to keep their efforts fresh against the Persians. This was doubtless an essential policy if resistance was going to be sustained over any period – although the Persians had not been able to establish a tactical advantage, the grinding effects of attrition and exhaustion were still on their side, if the battle played out over time.

Yet away from the immediate battlefield, the second day brought a crucial development, sown in the act of betrayal. Lured by the promise of riches, one Ephialtes, a local man familiar with the coastline and mountainous interior, approached Xerxes and promised information about a route by which the

The Spartan attack

In this scene, from the first day of fighting between Spartans and Persians at Thermopylae, the Spartans make a strong foray out from the Phocian Wall, driving back the Persians who had made the initial failed assaults. The Phocian Wall gave the Spartans an extremely useful physical feature for presenting their ranks across a narrow front, thereby obviating the Persian advantage in numbers (the Persians could only attack across the same breadth of front as that occupied by the Greeks), but offensive attacks as well as defensive actions were key to the Spartan resistance on the coastal road. Here the Spartans keep, to some degree, the classic structure of the hoplite phalanx, the shield-bearing men providing an interlocking, or at least supportive, defence to those on either side. In the reality of battle, however, ranks would often spread out and become ragged, as shown here. Furthermore, the primary hoplite weapon – the *dory* – was

probably more effectively wielded with some degree of space to drive it forward and target opponents to the sides. Some of the Spartans here have lost their spears; such losses typically occurred when spears became embedded in thick shields, or had their tips broken off from sword strikes or impact against metal armour or heavy shields. As soon as this happened, the Spartan would resort to using his *xiphos* sword. The Persians here are crumbling under the Spartan push. *Sparabara* heavy infantry at the front attempt to hold back the drive with their large wicker shields, sufficient to stop light blows but not a full-force spear thrust, while Persian infantry fight back with their battle-axes. The famous Persian archers still look for gaps in the Spartan ranks, seeking close-quarters targets. Essentially the scene shows a clash between two systems: the classic Greek hoplite phalanx, and the lighter, more combined-arms approach of the Persians.

Spartans could be outflanked. This was the Anopaia Path, which ran inland from the West Gate, through the Asopus Gorge, up along the Kallidromos Mountains and then down to Alpenoi on the coast, behind the East Gate. Ephialtes promised that he would act as a guide to the Persians along the route. In this opportunistic act, Ephialtes would bring down the Spartan resistance.

On the morning of the third day of battle, it was time for Xerxes to play his new ace card. During the previous night, his Immortals, led by Hydarnes, had worked their way along the Anopaia Path – no mean feat in the dark. The path was treacherous in parts, and oak trees and bushes loomed constantly out of the darkness. Yet by the first hints of daybreak, the Persians were emerging onto the flatter lands inland from Thermopylae.

It was here that they met the Phocian rearguard, an encounter that prompted a startled action, each side improvising with their attack and defence. Herodotus explains both the reasons for the complete surprise achieved by the Persians, and the subsequent fighting:

The Phocians learned in the following way that the Persians had climbed up: they had ascended without the Phocians' notice because the mountain was entirely covered with oak trees. Although there was no wind, a great noise arose like leaves being trodden underfoot. The Phocians jumped up and began to put on their weapons, and in a moment the barbarians were there. When they saw the men arming themselves, they were amazed, for they had supposed that no opposition would appear, but they had now met with an army. Hydarnes feared that the Phocians might be Lacedaemonians and asked Epialtes what country the army was from. When he had established what he wanted to know with certainty, he arrayed the Persians for battle. The Phocians, assailed by thick showers of arrows and supposing that the Persians had set out against them from the start, fled to the top of the mountain and prepared to meet their destruction. This is what they

intended, but the Persians with Epialtes and Hydarnes paid no attention to the Phocians and went down the mountain as fast as possible. (Herodotus VII.218)

Rather than be drawn into a casualty-inducing action prior to the assault on the Spartans, the Persian flanking force instead sidelined the Phocians in the terrain, bypassing and isolating them and thereby rendering them completely irrelevant to the subsequent action.

Leonidas, meanwhile, had been informed by lookouts that the Persians were now advancing from his rear – sobering information darkened even further, if Herodotus is to be believed, by the seer Megistias giving Leonidas the encouraging news that death was approaching at daybreak. In a defining moment of command, Leonidas knew that the Middle Gate would be lost, so he ordered his allies (apart from the Thespians and Thebans) to retreat. The Spartans would hold the pass as a rearguard, until their inevitable destruction.

As the sunlight painted itself across the landscape on the morning of that third day, the Spartans ate breakfast – Leonidas noting that it would be their last meal – and underwent the historical Spartan rituals of combing their long hair, a practice noted by Xerxes when he first encountered the Spartans. Across the lines, the Persians also readied themselves, and Herodotus takes up the narrative:

Xerxes made libations at sunrise and waiting till about mid-morning, made his assault. Epialtes had advised this, for the descent from the mountain is more direct, and the way is much shorter than the circuit and ascent. Xerxes and his

ABOVE LEFT
Hoplite figures are often represented as fighting naked. Such depictions frequently stem from the heroic Greek associations with nudity, but it is certainly true that some armies fought in very light clothing, particularly the Spartans. (PHAS/Universal Images Group/Getty Images)

ABOVE RIGHT
A statue of Leonidas I, king of Sparta and posthumous hero of the battle of Thermopylae. The statue is a modern one (1960s), but it captures well many of the components of the Spartan equipment: the Corinthian helmet, the muscle cuirass and the shin greaves. (PHAS/Universal Images Group/Getty Images)

barbarians attacked, but Leonidas and his Hellenes, knowing they were going to their deaths, advanced now much farther than before into the wider part of the pass. In all the previous days they had sallied out into the narrow way and fought there, guarding the defensive wall. Now, however, they joined battle outside the narrows and many of the barbarians fell, for the leaders of the companies beat everyone with whips from behind, urging them ever forward. Many of them were pushed into the sea and drowned; far more were trampled alive by each other, with no regard for who perished. Since the Hellenes knew that they must die at the hands of those who had come around the mountain, they displayed the greatest strength they had against the barbarians, fighting recklessly and desperately. (Herodotus VII.223)

This vivid account shows how the Spartans continued to bring fight and defiance to the battlefield, inflicting great casualties on the Persians in close-quarters combat, at which the Spartans excelled. (The Spartans regarded the missile-related skills of the Persians, such as archery, slinging and javelin-hurling, as cowardly, and certainly implying a barbaric lack of martial nobility.) It is notable that at this stage of the battle Leonidas brought his hoplites out of the narrow part of the pass to a wider point, meaning that all his men were now committed to the fight across a broader front – conservation of energy was no longer a priority. The intensity of the fighting, which continued for more than an hour, resulted in most of the Spartan spears being lost or shattered. Resorting to the sword, Leonidas ordered a pitifully

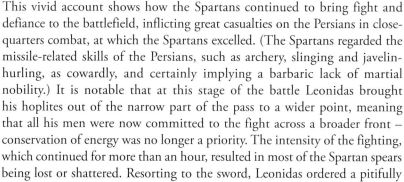

A grave *stele* of a hoplite named 'Aristion'. Such markers were a poignant remembrance of soldiers fallen in war; in some circumstances, soldiers might be buried en masse on the battlefield in what effectively became consecrated ground. (Jebulon/Wikimedia/CC0 1.0)

spirited charge against the enemy, but during the mêlée Leonidas himself was killed. This event in itself galvanized the Spartans, who fought in a futile frenzy to reclaim the king's body, which they did after having shoved the Persians back no fewer than four times.

But now Hydarnes and the Immortals had emerged from behind the Spartans and the surviving Thespians and Thebans, and added their weight of missile to the battle. The Spartans, few in number, now retreated to the hillock of Kolonos, just east of the Phocian Gate, for their last stand. At this point the Thebans – who had actually stayed with Leonidas under compulsion, as hostages (unlike the volunteer Thespians) – threw away their weapons and attempted to surrender to Xerxes, but the callousness induced by battle meant that many were killed out of hand by the vengeful Persians. The Spartans, weakened by wounds and immense fatigue, their weapons broken, were then destroyed to a man by merciless showers of arrows from both front and rear.

Xerxes had his victory, but at an immense cost that must have gut-punched his

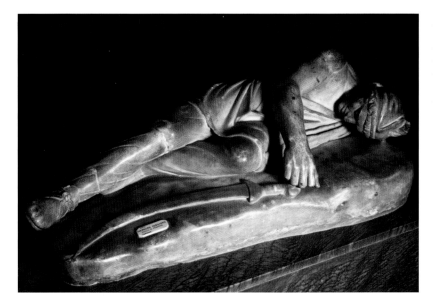

confidence. Herodotus states that at least 20,000 Persians were killed; we should treat this as a possible exaggeration, but still see it as an indication of the magnitude of the Persian withering. Furthermore, Herodotus observes that

> Many famous Persians also fell there, including two sons of Darius, Abrocomes and Hyperanthes, born to Darius by Phratagune daughter of Artanes. Artanes was the brother of king Darius and son of Hystaspes son of Arsames. When he gave his daughter in marriage to Darius, he gave his whole house as dowry, since she was his only child. Two brothers of Xerxes accordingly fought and fell there. (Herodotus VII.224–25)

The personal loss suffered by Xerxes, and the general military humiliation, become apparent in his contemptuous disrespect for the bodies of his foes, and particularly that of their leader:

> Having spoken in this way, Xerxes passed over the place where the dead lay and hearing that Leonidas had been king and general of the Lacedaemonians, he gave orders to cut off his head and impale it. It is plain to me by this piece of evidence among many others, that while Leonidas lived, king Xerxes was more incensed against him than against all others; otherwise he would never have dealt so outrageously with his dead body, for the Persians are beyond all men known in the habit of honoring valiant warriors. (Herodotus VII.238)

Herodotus' accounts are never to be taken entirely at face value, although in many cases they are the best that we have and at least seem anchored in some depth of historical seriousness, rather than pure invention. Thermopylae has, not least in recent times, been invested with such a heroic grandeur that it can be difficult to sense the more brutal and basic truths of that battle some 2,500 years ago. Yet the birth of such a legendary narrative does not seem possible had not, in 480 BC, a small group of men left a lasting impression on a mighty enemy with its vulnerabilities exposed.

Plataea

479 BC

BACKGROUND TO BATTLE

The battle of Thermopylae had been a glorious defeat for the Greeks, but a defeat nevertheless. Xerxes remained in possession of a vast army, despite the loss of 20,000 men from its ranks, and also retained the will to subjugate Greece and its troublesome peoples. The Persian advance through northern Greece continued with force.

The Athenians, while possessing a sizeable land army and a potent navy, nevertheless saw – clarified by dire Delphic oracles – that the Persian taking of Athens was inevitable. Therefore, in the summer of 480 BC, the city's council decreed that

> The whole of the Athenians and the foreigners who live in Athens shall move their wives and children to Troizen ... and their old folk and moveable property to Salamis ... All the rest of the Athenians and the resident foreigners who have reached manhood shall embark on the 200 ships prepared and fight against the barbarians for the sake of their own freedom and that of the other Greeks. (Quoted in Souza 2003: 59–60)

Athens was abandoned to the reckless vengeance of the Persians, who swept through Boeotia and Attica, then occupied and torched the city – the Athenians watched the fires from Salamis – as well as slaughtering many people in the surrounding countryside.

Yet within the Athenian decree of retreat, there was a sense of hope in the country's naval strength. The Hellenic League had shown at the battle of Artemisium, fought simultaneously with Thermopylae, that the Greek triremes could take on the might of the Persian navy. Then at

Pausanias

Like Mardonius, Pausanias had the highest royal associations. He was the son of Cleombrotus, regent of Sparta between 480 and 479 BC, and nephew of Leonidas I. Pausanias continued in his father's footsteps by becoming the Spartan regent on the death of Leonidas at the battle of Thermopylae. Details about Pausanias' background are scant, but we do know that he took command of the force at Plataea in his twenties, his relative youth as a general perhaps reflected in some of the many debates among the Greek commanders on the Plataean battlefield (although generalship in the ancient world was often a discursive process, rather than simply a matter of hierarchical decree). Nevertheless, his handling of the victory at Plataea showed that he had a measure of tactical assurance, backed by what appears to be a pious character, consulting sacrificial omens even during the most intensive parts of the battle. Yet, and allowing for the bias of Herodotus and Thucydides, he is also presented as a somewhat arrogant soul. Following Plataea, he was charged in 478 BC with conspiring with the Persians. He was acquitted of the charge, but his relationship with the Persians remained problematic, and he eventually died of starvation while hiding from arrest by the Spartan ephors.

Salamis, in early September 480 BC the Greeks inflicted a defeat of such magnitude that it arguably had a shaping effect on the very course and nature of Western history. Xerxes decided that time and patience were now the weapons of choice, and his army began the long retreat north. In fact, Xerxes realized that his campaign against Greece would be renewed with the return of favourable weather the following year (ancient societies were largely agrarian, therefore wars tended to be seasonal affairs to cooperate with crop cycles). Thus he left the bulk of his army, under the command of his cousin Mardonius, to winter in Thessaly, while the much-reduced Persian fleet sailed back across the Aegean Sea for its safe anchorage in Asia Minor. The Athenians moved back into their gaunt city and began rebuilding, but with the shadow of Mardonius' army falling long and deep over southern Greece from its positions further north, it must have been an uneasy autumn and winter.

In the spring of 479 BC, Xerxes' campaign to absorb Greece awoke from its winter hibernation. At first the activity was primarily political – Mardonius sent envoys to the Greek states dangling various carrots, encouraging compliance over certain defeat. The Athenians vigorously rejected the propositions, and so Mardonius quickly switched to the stick, marching his army south and once again taking an Athens quickly abandoned by its people. The Athenian leadership entered into bitter communications with Sparta, accusing the Spartans of now leaving Attica to its fate. Thinly veiled Athenian threats of a Persian alliance appear to have galvanized the Spartans into action, marching out through the Greek isthmus with 5,000 Spartan warriors plus a similar number of *periokoi* (citizens of Laconia and Messenia, Spartan allies) and each accompanied by a militarily and logistically useful helot. On the journey, they were joined by thousands of Greek allies which, when united with the Athenians' 8,000 hoplites and the 600 Plataeans, meant that the Hellene army now included more than 41,000 hoplites, plus thousands of other lightly armed troops, ultimately commanded by the Spartan Pausanias.

Mardonius now felt the threat of the combined might of Greece. Fearing that his forces might be trapped in Attica, and seeking more advantageous terrain to utilize his large and more mobile army (at least

Mardonius

By the time he led the Persian army at Plataea in 479 BC, Mardonius already had a chequered military career behind him. His regal family connections – Darius I married his sister and Mardonius' father, Gobryas, married Darius' sister – led to a political high profile and major army commands. In 492 BC, Mardonius was given charge of Persian forces charged with crushing the Ionian Revolt. Although Mardonius had much success on land, he was seriously wounded in battle and his command of the Persian invasion fleet was blighted when hundreds of ships were lost in a storm off the Greek coast near Mount Athos. He was not given command of the Persians for the 490 BC campaign, but his influence grew following the ascension of Xerxes I in 486 BC. From 485 BC, Mardonius was back at the head of the troops, first in Egypt then once again in Greece, one of six generals leading Persian forces there. Mardonius' defeat and death at Plataea is presented by Herodotus as the final destination for the general's hubris, ambition and defiance of the gods (crossing the Asopus River contrary to advice from the seers). Viewed more impartially, though, Mardonius ran on the whole an effective campaign in Greece, sacking Athens twice and, until the defeat at Plataea, stamping his authority over much of Greece north of the Isthmus.

compared to that of the enemy), he decided to move his troops out into Boeotia. Once again Athens was relinquished. Mardonius first took his men directly north through Archanes and up to Deceleia, then hooked west around Mount Parnes and began following the line of the Asopus River, eventually stopping on the north bank and building a fort there for his army, opposite Mount Cithaeron south of the river, there awaiting the Greeks.

The Greeks themselves also advanced up through Boeotia, but instead the allied army convened near Eleusis before heading north up through the Thriasian Plain. They moved up and over Mount Cithaeron via Eleutherae, placing themselves in the mountain's foothills just east of the town of Plataea.

This scene from the Nereid Monument of Xanthos, c.400 BC, provides a flattened image of Greek hoplites under attack while marching into action in formation, the soldiers close enough to one another to find protection from the adjacent *aspis* shields. (Christophel Fine Art/ Universal Images Group/Getty Images)

MAP KEY

1 The Greek and the Persian forces form up on the battlefield, with the Persians north of the Asopus River and the Greeks stretched out through the foothills of the Cithaeron range. They may have remained in these positions for several days.

2 The Persians are the first to make a move. Cavalry under the command of Masistius move forward from their positions around the Persian fort, cross the Asopus, and gather for an assault, moving out beyond the protection of their infantry.

3 The Persian cavalry make a number of wheeling attacks across the Greek lines. The Megarians on the Greek left are the most threatened of the Greek formations, but the lines broadly hold.

4 Athenian forces, and particularly a force of 300 archers, wheel inward against the Persian cavalry onslaught. The archers inflict particularly heavy casualties on the enemy, who are compelled to retreat.

5 Following the first day of battle, there is about a week without fighting. During this time, the Greeks adjust their lines, moving up to the southern edge of the Asopus to face the Persians, who move up to just across the river.

6 Breaking the period of stand-off, the Persian cavalry makes a sweeping incursion against the Greek right. The most devastating part of the action is a pincer attack against the largely undefended Greek supply column moving up towards Hysiae. The column suffers heavy casualties and vital supplies are destroyed.

7 One element of the Persian cavalry also swings out to foul the Greek water supply at the Gargaphia Spring.

8 Responding to the Persian cavalry attacks, overnight the Greek centre pulls back to the area known as 'the Island',
just in front of Plataea, to give it a more defensible position, shortening its line in the process. The move is meant to be part of a general Greek pull-back, but it is uncoordinated.

9 The Greek right begins its own withdrawal just before sunrise, although a Spartan unit under Amompharetus delays its withdrawal until later in the morning.

10 Persian cavalry forces in the centre launch an assault against the Greek right, at the moment that Amompharetus' unit joins the rest of the force. The Greeks draw into a close formation against the wheeling cavalry attacks, defending themselves behind a shield wall.

11 The units on the Greek left attempt to cross the battlefield to provide support to the beleaguered Greek right, but they are intercepted on the way by infantry forces from the Persian right. The two forces join combat around Asopus Ridge.

12 Persian infantry forces advance forward to attack the Greek right. They relieve the Persian cavalry, who have been maintaining a continual assault, allowing the cavalry to wheel back to equip themselves with more arrows and javelins.

13 Eventually, the Greek right moves from the defence to the attack, driving forward in a solid assault that pushes back the Persian and barbarian infantry in front of it. The Persian forces in this sector crumble, and they flee back to the fort beyond the Asopus River, with medizing Greek cavalry retarding the pace of the Greek advance.

14 The troops of the Greek centre and left also manage to break the Persian attacks and begin to advance. The Persian right also flees back across the Asopus, but flanking attacks from Persian cavalry mean that the Greeks push forward only with heavy losses.

Battlefield environment

The Plataean battlefield was a gently undulating grassy plain framed to the north by the Asopus River, running in a west–east orientation, and in the south by Mount Cithaeron. Six ridges ran down from the mountain to the plain, transitioning from the steep heights of the mountain down to gentle foothills running into the flatlands below. The two ridges that dominated the Plataean battlefield were the Pyrgos Ridge, furthest west, and the larger Asopus Ridge. The town of Plataea itself sat at the western base of the Asopus Ridge; other centres of habitation included the village of Hysiae (with its nearby Temple of Demeter) on the opposite side of the Asopus Ridge, and further east the village of Erythrae. Criss-crossing the battlefield were a series of roads and streams. The road network linked Plataea, Hysiae and Erythrae, two roads from the west converging on Hysiae into a single road, while two other roads ran directly towards Attica on a north–south axis, moving through the mountain passes. Plataea also had a north-leading road running out of the town – all the roads running out north from Plataea went into Thebes. The battlefield's waterways had a shaping effect on the battle, providing both defensive attributes plus, critically, hydration for tens of thousands of men baking under the Greek sun. For the Greeks, the Gargaphia Spring, located on the Asopus Ridge, was of particular importance. During the battle, the Persian cavalry would foul this water supply and use archery to deny the Greeks access to it.

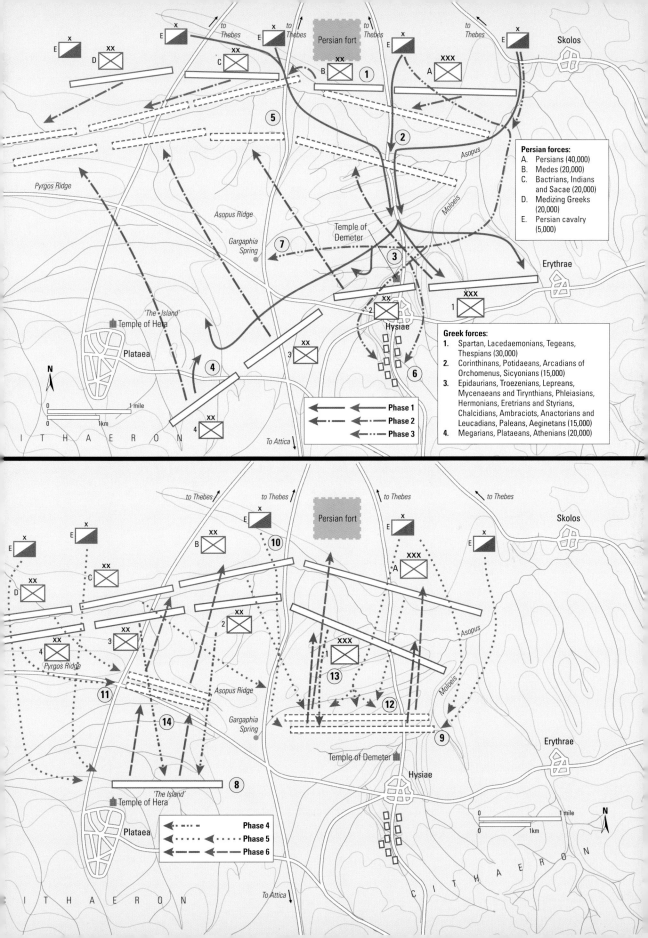

Persian forces:
A. Persians (40,000)
B. Medes (20,000)
C. Bactrians, Indians and Sacae (20,000)
D. Medizing Greeks (20,000)
E. Persian cavalry (5,000)

Greek forces:
1. Spartan, Lacedaemonians, Tegeans, Thespians (30,000)
2. Corinthinans, Potidaeans, Arcadians of Orchomenus, Sicyonians (15,000)
3. Epidaurians, Troezenians, Lepreans, Mycenaeans and Tirynthians, Phleiasians, Hermonians, Eretrians and Styrians, Chalcidians, Ambraciots, Anactorians and Leucadians, Paleans, Aeginetans (15,000)
4. Megarians, Plataeans, Athenians (20,000)

Phase 1
Phase 2
Phase 3

Phase 4
Phase 5
Phase 6

Skolos

Persian fort

to Thebes
to Thebes
to Thebes
to Thebes

Erythrae

Asopus
Moloeis

Pyrgos Ridge
Asopus Ridge
Gargaphia Spring
Temple of Demeter
Hysiae

'The Island'
Temple of Hera
Plataea

N

0   1 mile
0   1km

To Attica

C I T H A E R O N

INTO COMBAT

Having arrived at the Plataean plain and industriously built a large fort/camp there, Mardonius arranged his *c.*100,000 infantry in linear fashion north of the river in four main divisions, each according to ethnicity. From the Persian left to right these divisions were: the Persians themselves (*c.*40,000 men); the warrior-like Medes (20,000); Bactrians, Indians and Sacae (20,000); and a 20,000-strong force of 'medizing' Greeks, who had allied themselves to the Persian juggernaut. Behind the infantry, and extending out to the far left and right flanks, were five units of Persian cavalry totalling 5,000 men and mounts, and constituting Mardonius' mobile arm of decision.

The Greeks, meanwhile, took up opposing positions in the foothills of the Cithaeron Mountains, their formations extending between Erythrae and Plataea. As fighting positions, the lower slopes had their merits, the upward slope of the land giving a natural defensive advantage while a good road network and reliable water sources meant that the men could be kept fed and hydrated in readiness. Mardonius, having allowed the Greeks to form up some 5km away from the Persian positions, now decided to test the mettle of his enemy. He deployed his cavalry, commanded by Masistius, across the Asopus River to make a harassing attack in force, probing the Greek lines with repeated sweeping assaults, trying to find the weak points. It was the Megarians, on the Greek left, who took the heaviest blows, and an appeal for help from the neighbouring Athenians was answered by a force of 300 hand-picked warriors including, crucially, Greek archers. The Athenian archers sent a lethal hail of arrows into the Persian men and beasts, the wounded and dismounted – including Masistius himself – finished off by the hoplites. Herodotus gives a darkly graphic account of the events surrounding Masistius' death:

> The cavalry charged by squadrons, and Masistius' horse, being at the head of the rest, was struck in the side by an arrow. Rearing up in pain, it threw Masistius, who when he fell, was straightaway set upon by the Athenians. His horse they took then and there, and he himself was killed fighting. They could not, however, kill him at first, for he was outfitted in the following manner: he wore a purple tunic over a cuirass of golden scales which was within it; thus they accomplished nothing by striking at the cuirass, until someone saw what was happening and stabbed him in the eye. Then he collapsed and died. But as chance would have it, the rest of the horsemen knew nothing of this, for they had not seen him fall from his horse, or die. They wheeled about and rode back without perceiving what was done. As soon as they halted, however, they saw what they were missing since there was no one to give them orders. Then when they perceived what had occurred, they gave each other the word, and all rode together to recover the dead body. (Herodotus IX.22)

So it was that the first day of combat was a victory for the Greeks, and Pausanias now felt confident enough to move his forces forward, along the line of the Pyrgos and Asopus ridges. Herodotus explains in detail the organization and composition of the Greek forces:

> Presently the whole Greek army was arrayed as I will show, both the later and the earliest comers. On the right wing were ten thousand Lacedaemonians; five

thousand of these, who were Spartans, had a guard of thirty-five thousand light-armed helots, seven appointed for each man. The Spartans chose the Tegeans for their neighbors in the battle, both to do them honor, and for their valor; there were of these fifteen hundred men-at-arms. Next to these in the line were five thousand Corinthians, at whose desire Pausanias permitted the three hundred Potidaeans from Pallene then present to stand by them. Next to these were six hundred Arcadians from Orchomenus, and after them three thousand men of Sicyon. By these one thousand Troezenians were posted, and after them two hundred men of Lepreum, then four hundred from Mycenae and Tiryns, and next to them one thousand from Phlius. By these stood three hundred men of Hermione. Next to the men of Hermione were six hundred Eretrians and Styreans; next to them, four hundred Chalcidians; next again, five hundred Ampraciots. After these stood eight hundred Leucadians and Anactorians, and next to them two hundred from Pale in Cephallenia; after them in the array, five hundred Aeginetans; by them stood three thousand men of Megara, and next to these six hundred Plataeans. At the end, and first in the line, were the Athenians who held the left wing. They were eight thousand in number, and their general was Aristides son of Lysimachus. All these, except the seven appointed to attend each Spartan, were men-at-arms, and the whole sum of them was thirty-eight thousand and seven hundred. (Herodotus IX.28–29)

In Herodotus' account, which doubtless includes excessive numbers (especially in relation to the 35,000 helots), he also devotes space to describing an argument between the Athenians and the Tegeans, about who should have the right to occupy the prestigious left flank of the line. The debate was apparently won by the Athenians, by listing their martial achievements.

We have already witnessed, at both Marathon and Thermopylae, the role that inactivity could play in the Greek and Persian Wars, and Plataea was no exception. For a period of about a week, the two sides simply faced one another, each possibly hoping to force the hand of the other through stand-off. It was Mardonius who broke the status quo. During a night-time operation, his left-flank cavalry were sent clear around the Greek right to attack the Greek supply line running through the Cithaeron Pass. It was an inspired move. In the early morning, just below Hysiae, the cavalry unleashed their dreadful surprise on a supply column of 500 carts and pack animals, slaughtering both men and beasts without compunction.

The Greeks were now running low on supplies, plus they had a growing threat to their rear. Two days after the supply-line disaster, the Persian cavalry began launching repeated incursions into the Greek lines, snatching away lives through arrow and javelin. They also achieved a further logistical victory, reaching and fouling the Gargaphia Spring, a critical Greek water source. Although the cavalry could be kept at bay, Herodotus is clear about the concern now sweeping through the Greek ranks:

> … seeing that their army was cut off from water and thrown into confusion by the horsemen, the generals of the Greeks went to Pausanias on the right wing, and debated concerning this and other matters; for there were other problems which troubled them more than what I have told. They had no food left, and their followers whom they had sent into the Peloponnese to bring provisions had been cut off by the horsemen and could not make their way to the army. (Herodotus IX.50)

Under pressure, the Greeks now sought to rationalize their lines. Herodotus explains that the decision was taken to pull back to 'the Island', a defensible area of land in front of Plataea town delineated by two channels of the river running down from Mount Cithaeron. The rivers would provide defence against the Persian cavalry, and they would

also solve the water-shortage problem following the loss of the Gargaphia Spring. The exact location of the Island has been blurred by history and geographical change, but the basic principle was that the Greeks were shortening and strengthening their lines of defence between Hysiae and Plataea.

The movement back to the new positions was conducted with some chaos, and consequently opened cracks in the Greek formations that the Persians then sought to exploit in the final decisive battle. Overnight, the Greek centre began to pull back, but one of the Spartan divisions, commanded by a certain Amompharetus, initially refused the retreat, seeing it as ignoble. He was eventually persuaded to comply, but the overall Greek retreat was slowed in waiting for the Spartan division to catch up. The

In this Classical Greek sculpture, we witness the divinity Heracles killing Cycnus, son of Ares. As is often the way with mythological Greek scenes, martial details are revealed; in this image, note the *agave* grip on the *aspis* shield, with the elbow passing through the *porpax* central band and the hand gripping the *antilabe* strap at the rim. (Christophel Fine Art/Universal Images Group/Getty Images)

This useful frieze image shows two *xiphos* swords in their scabbards with the suspension cord fitting, which would have looped up and over the warrior's right shoulder to suspend the sword on his left hip. (DEA/G. DAGLI ORTI/De Agostini/ Getty Images)

Athenians on the opposite flank also did not pull back as expected, while the central division went back further than planned.

As dawn broke, and the Persians were able to see the Greek retreat unfolding before them, Mardonius realized that the moment of decision had arrived, despite the advice of one of his commanders, Artabazus, that they should take this moment to retreat back to Thebes. Mardonius' first act was to unleash his Persian cavalry in the centre, the mounted troops sweeping through the now-vacated Greek central positions to attack the Spartan right just as Amompharetus' men were joining up with the main body. This fast attack threatened to break the integrity of the Greek line – a disastrous prospect given that the Greeks were almost exclusively a hoplite force, and unified ranks were at the heart of their fighting capability. The Spartans immediately closed up, the Persian cavalry wheeling about them, the Persian infantry firing arrows from distance. Mardonius then also unleashed his infantry against the Greek right, the screaming mob of warriors racing forward with swords, spears and bows at the ready.

An ornate ivory sword chape (the fitting that caps the end of a scabbard), dating from the Hellenistic era, depicting the struggle between Greeks and Amazons. (Werner Forman/Universal Images Group/Getty Images)

With the bulk of the Persian attack thundering down upon the Spartans, the Athenians began to move across the battlefront to go to their aid. This movement, however, was intercepted by the medizing Greeks, and fierce infantry combat ensued behind the Asopus Ridge. Yet it was still the Lacedaemonians and Tegeans who reeled under the heaviest attacks; once the Persian cavalry retreated to replenish their arrows and javelins, the Greek right spent many shuddering minutes beneath their shields under a rainstorm of arrows and other missiles. They withstood the pressure with the same tenacity they had shown at Thermopylae, and then, when Pausanias was looking for divine salvation, they went on the attack:

> Since the Spartans were being hard-pressed and their sacrifices were of no avail, Pausanias lifted up his eyes to the temple of Hera at Plataea and called on the goddess, praying that they might not be disappointed in their hope. While he was still in the act of praying, the men of Tegea leapt out before the rest and charged the barbarians, and immediately after Pausanias' prayer the sacrifices of the Lacedaemonians became favourable. Now they too charged the Persians, and the Persians met them, throwing away their bows. First they fought by the fence of shields, and when that was down, there was a fierce and long fight around the temple of Demeter itself, until they came to blows at close quarters. For the barbarians laid hold of the spears and broke them short. Now the Persians were

The Greek advance

Greek view: On the last day of fighting at Plataea, hoplite forces on the Greek left flank, having pushed through Boeotian resistance, advance in an arrayed phalanx against the Persian lines that have retreated across the Asopus River. The scene illustrates the core differences between the Greek and Persian approaches to warfare at this time. The Greeks drive forward behind their *aspis* shields, while clutching their spears, the front rank preparing to stand after riding out cavalry and archery assaults from the knee. Note how the close integrity of the shield wall fragments in places as the soldiers move forward, adjusting their steps and pace to deal with the terrain and opening gaps of opportunity for enemy spearmen and archers. Persian arrows thump into the Greek shields, but even at close range the arrows were rarely able to penetrate the thick wood. The biggest threat to the hoplites is the flanking attacks made by Persian cavalry (shown here in the background to the left); the wheeling javelin attacks from the cavalry inflicted serious casualties on the Greek soldiers, who struggled to orient their shields to face such attacks, and the cavalry prevented the last day of the Plataea fighting being a complete Persian rout.

Persian view: This view of the battle illustrates the looser fighting order of the Persians, when compared to that of the Greeks. *Sparabara* heavy infantry, protected behind their wicker shields and armed with *c.*1.8m spears, provide a defensive front to the formation, but mixed with light infantry armed with bows, swords and axes. Through the gaps in the shield wall, archers conduct close-range direct fire but also high-angle indirect fire from further back, attempting to inflict attrition from a distance. Light infantry fight with small shields for protection and axes and swords for the attack. The short battle-axe, in trained hands, had a versatile range of motion, being able to attack target points on the enemy from the ankles up to the head. The pick-head fitting was particularly useful for hacking down the Greek shields, splintering the wood and dragging down the top of the shield to expose the hoplite to sword, bow and spear attacks. At close quarters, however, the relative lack of Persian body armour and the short fighting radius of the sword and the axe meant that the Persians were often disadvantaged against the long reach of the *dory*. In this view we also see a Persian cavalryman unleashing a javelin at the exposed Greek flank, just before wheeling away. The cavalryman also carries a bow; the short Persian recurve bows were ideal for horse-archery, being convenient to wield from horseback and offering an effective range of more than 100m, even while the horse was in motion.

neither less valorous nor weaker, but they had no armor; moreover, since they were unskilled and no match for their adversaries in craft, they would rush out singly and in tens or in groups great or small, hurling themselves on the Spartans and so perishing. (Herodotus IX.61–62)

Now, once again, began the collapse of the Persian ranks. The Spartans, locking into the *othismos*, drove back their less-disciplined opponents in inching close-quarters combat, the close proximity to the enemy partly undoing the Persians' advantage in archery. Some time later, the Athenians on the left flank also achieved a momentum in advance, although a persistent Persian fight-back drove them back to the Cithaeron Mountains. The Persians managed some measure of control in retreat. The cavalry kept wheeling in to retard the drive of the Greek attack. Indeed, a medized Theban cavalry counter-attack against the now-advancing Greek centre resulted in heavy losses for the Greeks. The efforts of the cavalry also allowed many Persian infantry to pull back inside the temporary safety of the fort.

Eventually, the Persians were driven from the battlefield, the collapse gathering momentum when Mardonius was killed in action. Many of the Persians fled north, while the fort was placed under siege by the Athenians, as the Spartans had little knowledge of siege warfare. The walls were finally breached by the Tegeans, allowing Greek forces to stream inside the camp and unleash a heavy slaughter on the demoralized and exhausted Persians.

The Greeks carried the day in the battle of Plataea. As always, accurate casualty figures are an impossibility, given the variation between the sources. A synthesis and interpretation of the figures suggests Persian casualties of up to 90,000, while the Greeks lost fewer than 10,000, but such figures are merely informed guesses. What can be said with certainty, however, is that the Greeks had put a brutal cap on Persia's imperial ambitions.

ABOVE LEFT
A statuette of a hoplite, the spear in his hand having perished long ago. The angle of the shield is interesting, as this angle would have been difficult to maintain in a forward-pressing phalanx. Perhaps it shows the shield as it would have been held in the front ranks prior to the clash, or in more open-order fighting. (Hulton Archive/ Getty Images)

ABOVE RIGHT
A red-figure vase painting, most likely depicting *hoplitodromos*, of a hoplite wearing nothing but a helmet and carrying a shield. The lack of clothing might not be entirely artistic licence; although many hoplites are shown clad in metal and leather armour, some armies (such as the Spartans) might have indeed fought largely naked, or with little but a light and loose tunic for covering. (Bettmann/Getty Images)

Analysis

Although the battle of Thermopylae was ultimately a Persian victory, the three battles that constitute the heart of this book could, if removed from context, be taken to demonstrate the superiority of the Greek hoplite system among the ancient ways of war. If we come to such a conclusion, however, we are in danger of misreading the specific circumstances of each of these individual battles, plus isolating the engagements from the context of what happened subsequently.

Ultimately, hoplite warfare was developed to deliver maximum battlefield effect from a citizen-soldier army that, with obvious exceptions such as the Spartans, would have had limited military training and battlefield experience. The push, shove, stab and thrust of the hoplite phalanx had momentum, direction (although usually only one direction – forward) and compact killing force. But it also had its fair share of problems; particularly that noted earlier in this book – the issue of maintaining uniform ranks during the course of an advance over undulating or broken terrain. Added to this was the problem of right-hand drift, which Thucydides describes in this passage from his *History of the Peloponnesian Wars*:

> The Argives and their confederates marched to the charge with great violence and fury. But the Lacedaemonians slowly and with many flutes, according to their military discipline, not as a point of religion, but that, marching evenly and by measure, their ranks might not be distracted, as the greatest armies, when they march in the face of the enemy, use to be ... All armies do thus. In the conflict they extend their right wing so as it cometh in upon the flank of the left wing of the enemy: and this happeneth for that every one, through fear, seeketh all he can to cover his unarmed side with the shield of him that standeth next to him on his right hand, conceiving that to be so locked together is their best defence. The beginning hereof is in the leader of the first file on the right hand, who ever striving to shift his unarmed side from the enemy, the rest upon like fear follow after. (Thucydides V.70–71)

Essentially, as each hoplite closed up the gap with the soldier to his right, through his desire to protect himself, the entire hoplite rank made a steady drift in that direction, threatening to open up gaps between units or expose a flank. Add to this the other problems of the hoplite phalanx – issues with controlling weapons during a close-quarters *othismos*; lack of articulation to meet mobile threats; difficulties in command and control – and it can be quite difficult to see just why it was so persuasive on the battlefield.

The answer is that in many cases conditions had to be right to allow the hoplite phalanx to thrive. The Persian way of war, focusing mainly on archers backed by light infantry and cavalry, was very much a child of Near Eastern geography, with its vast areas of flat and open expanses. Here, flanks could be attacked easily, visibility was good for long-range archery and the numbers of troops were high, hence making the most of a small army was not a priority. In Greece, by contrast, the fighting terrain was often comprised of relatively small plains or plateaus between mountainous areas, and the armies were the diminutive ones of the *polis* – the army of an individual state might only number a few thousand troops. Therefore the hoplite phalanx thrived in the places of its birth, defined by terrain, training and limited tactical options.

The battles of Marathon and Thermopylae illustrate this point well. In both engagements, the landscape placed constraints on the action that prohibited the Persians from exploiting to their strengths, but allowed the Greeks to display the best of the hoplite force. The sea, marshes and woods at Marathon, and the coastal road, mountains, coastal cliffs, Phocian Wall and Malian Gulf at Thermopylae, all stopped the Persians sweeping around with their cavalry and instead compelled them to fight on a front that suited

A Greek hoplite locked in battle with the Amazons. The shield is the smaller and lighter (compared to the *aspis*) *pelte* variant, which had a crescent shape and was associated with the Thracian *peltasts*, light infantry made more salient in Greek armies through the Iphicratean reforms of the 4th century BC. (Print Collector/Hulton Archive/Getty Images)

Historically minded re-enactors have provided researchers with much useful practical information about how the Greek hoplites fought in the phalanx. In this image, for example, note the depth of coverage from the shield, from chin to lower thigh. (DEA/C. BALOSSINI/De Agostini/Getty Images)

the hoplite phalanx. We see a different dynamic at Plataea, where the greater expanse of the Plataean plain did permit the Persian cavalry to go hunting and exert a critical, and at times nearly decisive, influence upon the evolution of the battle. Only the tenacity of the Spartans, the intelligent use of defensive positions on the Cithaeron range, plus, tellingly, the Greeks' resort to their own missile troops to respond to the Persian cavalry, helped to tip the engagement in favour of a Greek victory.

Of course, the three battles considered here were far from the only ones fought by the Greeks during the Archaic and Classical eras, but many of the others were actually inter-Greek battles, in which hoplites faced opposing hoplites, both fighting within the familiarity of martial tradition. Yet although the Greek and Persian Wars did demonstrate how, under the right conditions, the hoplite phalanx could prevail, the wars implanted some new perspectives about the tactics and merits of light infantry, lessons that were reinforced by other conflicts in the remainder of the 5th century BC, including during the lengthy and costly Peloponnesian War (431–404 BC). For example, in 426 BC the Athenians invaded Aetolia, and were confronted with Aetolian javelin men, or *peltasts*. Unlike the heavily armoured hoplites, the *peltasts* wore only light clothing, hence they could move fast – far faster than a stolid hoplite. The Aetolian *peltasts* focused on staying out of range of the contingent of Greek archers that now accompanied the Athenian army. They waited until the archers' arrows were expended before rushing into javelin-throwing range, hurling their missiles into the Athenian ranks, then retreating rapidly. This they did, time and time again, the hoplites becoming maddeningly exhausted from their losses plus the sheer, futile effort of trying to catch the nimble-footed warriors.

Steadily, the Athenians and other Greek states began to develop and incorporate their own light infantry into their ranks. A major step forward came with what are known as the 'Iphicratean reforms' in the early 4th century BC, named after the eponymous general Iphicrates. It was the perceptive Iphicrates who incorporated the skills of Thracian and Paeonian *peltasts* – light skirmishers who had proved their worth as mercenaries fighting for the Persian Cyrus the Younger at Cunaxa in 401 BC – plus the lessons derived from the Persians themselves, into the Athenian army in the first half of the 4th century BC. The reforms were a mix of innovations in weaponry and tactics. The Athenian *peltasts* replaced the heavy *aspis* shield with a lighter round or crescent-shaped *pelte*, which could be strapped around the forearm to allow the soldier use of both hands for weaponry, if needed. Metal armour was largely replaced with linen or leather variants, making the soldier lighter on his feet. Spears and swords were lengthened, to give greater reach, and drills became more dynamic.

The proof of the potential of Iphicratean reforms was demonstrated in 392 BC, when the Athenian hoplite forces, commanded by Callias III but with support from Iphicrates and his *peltasts*, defeated Spartan hoplites at Corinth, as Xenophon recounts:

> Callias formed his hoplites in line of battle not far from the city, while Iphicrates with his peltasts attacked the Lacedaemonian regiment. Now when the Lacedaemonians were being attacked with javelins, and several men had been wounded and several others slain, they directed the shield-bearers to take up these wounded men and carry them back to Lechaeum; and these were the only men in the regiment who were really saved. Then the polemarch ordered the first ten year-classes to drive off their assailants. But when they pursued, they caught no one, since they were hoplites pursuing peltasts at the distance of a javelin's cast; for Iphicrates had given orders to the peltasts to retire before the hoplites got near them; and further, when the Lacedaemonians were retiring from the pursuit, being scattered because each man had pursued as swiftly as he could, the troops of Iphicrates turned about, and not only did those in front again hurl javelins upon the Lacedaemonians, but also others on the flank, running along to reach their unprotected side. Indeed, at the very first pursuit the peltasts shot down nine or ten of them. And as soon as this happened, they began to press the attack much more boldly. Then, as the Lacedaemonians continued to suffer losses, the polemarch again ordered the first fifteen year-classes to pursue. But when these fell back, even more of them were shot down than at the first retirement. (Xenophon, *Hellenica* IV.3.14–16)

With what must have been infuriating repetition, the Spartans here are locked into a brutal cycle of chase–loss–retreat, the Athenians utilizing the light infantry to superb effect, and fully illustrating the physical and tactical limitations of heavy infantry.

The hoplite model was shaken, but it would still be ingrained in the Greek martial psyche for centuries to come. What was happening, however,

This relief of Greek hoplites in battle gives a vivid impression of the close-quarters jostling involved as the shield walls collided. Note also how there could be a tendency for the pressure to be applied at an oblique angle, the shields sliding off each other and often causing formations to shift slightly to the right. (Photo by CM Dixon/Print Collector/Hulton Archive/ Getty Images)

was that the Greeks were learning from the encounters with the Persians, even from victories such as Marathon and Thermopylae, and starting to build a combined-arms approach into their forces. This found its ultimate expression in the campaigns of Philip II and then Alexander III of Macedon, the latter of whom through military conquest created an empire that exceeded the Persians' in terms of extent, and which in turn crushed Persian dominance on the battlefield. Philip established a force of heavy cavalry, armoured and equipped with shield and lance, to deliver mobile shock attacks through whole-unit articulated manoeuvres. The heavy cavalry was supplemented by faster javelin-armed light cavalry. Similarly, the infantry was divided into heavy and light types, the former receiving much longer spears to improve the stand-off distance with the enemy (and therefore reduce the need for heavy armour), while the light infantry provided skirmishing and missile attrition, and over time would become the more important of the infantry types.

Alexander was able to utilize these four elements of his army to impressive effect against the Persians, using manoeuvre to a degree that would have been unimaginable to the Greek forces of Marathon and Plataea. The Persians, already proponents of combined-arms warfare, found it particularly hard to resist the blows of the heavy cavalry, and also the ever-adaptive strategies of Alexander.

For above all else, the combined-arms approach to warfare relied on intelligent leadership. In the battles described in this book, there is a definite inflexibility in the tactics of the Greeks, who essentially looked to individual valour and the blunt instrument of the hoplite phalanx to press home their victory. In essence, the main function of the Greek military leader was to inspire the troops with martial spirit and religious sanction. The Persians under Mardonius demonstrated more innovation, particularly at Plataea with the sweeping cavalry attacks to the Greek rear and flanks, which were nearly the undoing of Pausanias' army. But it was Alexander who demonstrated the full capability of the combined-arms leadership, as well as the importance of an adaptive approach to battlefield tactics, as historian Archer Jones has described in his major work *The Art of War in the Western World*:

> Without Alexander's genius the Greeks could not have conquered the Persian Empire, but Alexander's masterful use of shock cavalry contributed importantly, perhaps decisively, to the tactical successes upon which the conquest depended. By a brilliant use of the four basic weapon systems, Alexander defeated the formidable Persians whose otherwise sophisticated tactical system did not include heavy cavalry. This significant Macedonian innovation completed the development of the basic tactical system that endured for many centuries. Alexander also advanced the art of war by his flexibility: he did not rely on a single disposition of his army for battle nor on a set-piece plan but adapted both plans and dispositions to the circumstances. (Jones 2001: 25–26)

Combined arms and tactical flexibility remain the governing principles of military tactics in today's modern armies. What Marathon, Thermopylae and Plataea demonstrated was the confrontation between a rather rigid and ritualistic Greek way of war, and more dynamic Persian tactics that, crucially, lacked the shock force later employed by Alexander. Without the fortunes provided by advantageous terrain, or the sheer will and dynamism of men such as the Spartans, the history of the Western world could have been quite different.

A mosaic representing the battle of Alexander III of Macedon (Alexander the Great) against Darius III, possibly at Issus or Gaugamela. The scene illustrates how far Alexander's army had developed a combined-arms approach compared to the earlier regimented lines of hoplites. (Museo Archeologico Nazionale, Naples/ Wikimedia/Public Domain)

Aftermath

While we can, with the benefit of hindsight, see some of the flaws in Greek hoplite warfare, and some of the strengths of Persian tactics, the fact remains that the battle of Plataea in 479 BC was an astounding victory for the Greeks. Although the Persians still left the Plataean battlefield with some 40,000 men under arms, Persian imperialism was critically wounded in Greece. Artabazus took the Persian troops straight back to Asia Minor, while the Hellene forces settled old scores. Pro-Persian Thebes came in for special attention – many Thebans had fought on the Persian side at Plataea, and Thebes itself provided a base to the rear from which the Persians could prosecute their campaign in Attica. In vengeance, the Greeks ransacked through the territories surrounding Thebes, and the city eventually fell after a three-week siege. Leading Thebans were executed for their lack of regional loyalty, and after this score was settled the Greek army was disbanded, the soldiers dispersing back to their individual states.

Sensing Persian weakness, and encouraged by the promise of naval support from the Hellenic League and the Greek destruction of the Persian fleet at Mycale in the summer of 479 BC, some coastal states in Ionia once again rebelled against Persian overlordship. The momentum of victory was now firmly behind the Greeks, and they turned their sights to Sestos, a critical Achaemenid port in the Thracian Chersonese that helped the Persians control the gateway to the Black Sea through the Hellespont. Led by the general Xanthippus – the commander of the Greek naval forces for the spectacular victory at Mycale – the Greeks placed Sestos under a prolonged siege, which finally ended with Persian capitulation in 478 BC. Pausanias also remained active against the Persians after Plataea. A naval expedition under his command stripped the Persians of most of Cyprus and all of Byzantium. Later, a new Greek alliance known as the Delian League, founded in 478 BC under Athenian leadership, continued campaigning against Xerxes' faltering empire. Over time, the Delian League managed to strip the eastern Aegean from Persian hands and inflicted some further epic blows in battle, including the great victory at Eurymedon in 469 or 466 BC.

A Persian relief sculpture shows Darius I enthroned, with his son Xerxes behind him. Neither man was able to tame the Greek mainland, which came to define the western limits of the Persian Empire. (Bettmann/Getty Images)

Perhaps a fitting place to end our narrative is 465 BC, with the assassination of Xerxes by Artabanus, the commander of the Persian royal bodyguard. Xerxes' successor, Artaxerxes I, faced no less of a challenge holding on to Persian territory than Xerxes himself, including having to quell an Athenian-support revolt in Egypt *c.*460 BC. Peace between the Persians and the Delian League, according to historical tradition, ended in 449 BC with the so-called Peace of Callias (although there is some debate about its existence); but by this time, new tensions had arisen in Greece between an increasingly imperialistic Athens and Sparta, leading to yet another round of bloodletting, in what would become the Peloponnesian War of 431–404 BC.

The Greek and Persian Wars of the 5th century BC were a formative moment both in cultural history (consider the redirection of Western history if the Greeks had been defeated) and also in military history. The wars brought together two very different styles of combat, in which the Greeks prevailed but also learned critical military lessons from the Persians for the future. For the best part of a century, the Greeks were able to build their reputation on the sheer violence and muscle of the hoplite soldier, still immortalized today in film and literature.

UNIT ORGANIZATIONS

Greek

The Greek hoplites were grouped according to a 'tribal' system, although this does not have the connotations of blood relations that it does in many other contexts. Essentially, the tribe was a politico-military grouping, with a similarity in principal to an electoral constituency. The example of 5th-century BC Attica provides us with a clear example of this structure. Based on the constitutional reforms of Cleisthenes in 508/07 BC, Attica was divided into three regions: *asty* – a city region; *paralia* – a coastal region; *mesogeia* – an inland region. From these regions, ten new *phylai* (tribes) were formed, each tribe composed of three *trittyes* or 'thirds', with one third taken from each of the regions. Each of the tribes, thus composed, was then given the name of a specific Greek hero. This tribal system connected directly to the organization of the hoplite army. Each *trittys* was obliged to provide a company of

300 hoplites, known as a *lochos*, thus each *phyle* yielded a total force of 900, which would then serve together as a unit on the battlefield. Each of the companies would be led by a *lochagos*, while each tribe had its own general; these men rotated through the command of the army during a campaign (according to Herodotus). Note that the tribes also had a sense of regional identity. Attica was subdivided into a large number of *deme* units, similar to the concept of a parish, and adjacent territories were grouped together locally in the formation of the *trittys*. Nicholas Sekunda also explains that 'Parish registers listing its citizens formed the basic documentation for elections and for military mobilization' (Sekunda 2002: 18). Thus it was that Athens was able to field a regional army of 9,000 hoplites, with each of the tribes carrying its own sense of identity and pride onto the battlefield.

Persian

The army of the Persian Empire was a vast entity containing literally dozens of ethnic forces, each with its own internal preferences for organization and leadership. Yet a centralized structure was applied to this potentially unwieldy mass, by use of a highly logical decimal system. The overarching unit of the Persian army was the *hazarabam*, meaning 'thousand', essentially a regiment of 1,000 men commanded by a leader known as a *hazarapatis*. Each of the *hazaraba* was then divided into manageable sub-units: ten *sataba* of 100, then ten *dathaba* of ten, with Xenophon (in his *Cyropaedia*) suggesting further subdivisions of five and 50. In this passage, Xenophon explains how Cyrus the Great 'observed that people are much more willing to practise those things in which they have rivalry among themselves, he appointed contests for them in everything that he knew it was important for soldiers to practise. What

he proposed was as follows: to the private soldier, that he show himself obedient to the officers, ready for hardship, eager for danger but subject to good discipline, familiar with the duties required of a soldier, neat in the care of his equipment, and ambitious about all such matters; to the corporal, that, besides being himself like the good private, he make his squad of five a model, as far as possible; to the sergeant, that he do likewise with his squad of ten, and the lieutenant with his platoon; and to the captain, that he be unexceptionable himself and see to it that the officers under him get those whom they command to do their duty' (Xenophon, *Cyropaedia* II.1.22). What we see here is a very traditional military sense of hierarchy, the minor units and their leadership reflecting (when everything was working properly) the order, pride and capability of the larger formations.

BIBLIOGRAPHY

Primary sources

Herodotus (440 BC). *The Histories*, trans. A.D. Godley. Cambridge, MA: Harvard University Press, 1920.

Plutarch (2nd century AD). *Plutarch's Lives*, trans. Bernadotte Perrin. Cambridge, MA: Harvard University Press & London: William Heinemann, 1914.

Strabo (*c*.7 BC). *The Geography of Strabo*, trans. H.C. Hamilton & W. Falconer. London: George Bell & Sons, 1903.

Thucydides (from 431 BC). *History of the Peloponnesian War*, trans. T. Hobbes. Chicago: University of Chicago Press, 1989.

Xenophon (*c*.370 BC). *Cyropaedia*, trans. Walter Miller. Cambridge, MA: Harvard University Press & London: William Heinemann, 1914.

Xenophon (4th century BC). *Hellenica*, trans. Carleton L. Brownson. Cambridge, MA: Harvard University Press & London: William Heinemann. Vol. 1, 1918; vol. 2, 1921.

Secondary sources

Bury, J.B. & Meiggs, Russell (1991). *A History of Greece*. London: Macmillan.

Campbell, Brian (2004). *Greek and Roman Military Writings: Selected Readings*. London & New York, NY: Routledge.

Campbell, Duncan B. (2012). *Spartan Warrior 735–331 BC*. Warrior 163. Oxford: Osprey Publishing.

Carey, Brian Todd, Allfree, Joshua B. & Cairns, John (2016). *Warfare in the Ancient World*. Barnsley: Pen & Sword.

Cassin-Scott, Jack (1977). *The Greek and Persian Wars 500–323 BC*. Men-at-Arms 69. London: Osprey Publishing.

Farrokh, Dr Kaveh (2007). *Shadows in the Desert: Ancient Persia at War*. Oxford: Osprey Publishing.

Fields, Nic (2007). *Thermopylae 480 BC: Last stand of the 300*. Campaign 188. Oxford: Osprey Publishing.

Fink, Dennis L. (2014). *The Battle of Marathon in Scholarship: Research, Theories and Controversies since 1850*. Jefferson, NC: McFarland & Co.

Jones, Archer (2001). *The Art of War in the Western World*. Urbana & Chicago, IL: University of Chicago Press.

Kagan, Donald & Viggiano, Gregory F., eds (2013). *Men of Bronze: Hoplite Warfare in Ancient Greece*. Princeton, NJ & Oxford: Oxford University Press.

Kitto, H.D.F. (1991). *The Greeks*. London: Penguin.

Sekunda, Nicholas (1992). *The Persian Army 560–330 BC*. Elite 42. Oxford: Osprey Publishing.

Sekunda, Nicholas (2000). *Greek Hoplite 480–323 BC*. Warrior 27. Oxford: Osprey Publishing.

Sekunda, Nicholas (2002). *Marathon 490 BC: The first Persian invasion of Greece*. Campaign 108. Oxford: Osprey Publishing.

Shepherd, William (2012). *Plataea 479 BC: The most glorious victory ever seen*. Campaign 239. Oxford: Osprey Publishing.

Souza, Philip de (2003). *The Greek and Persian Wars 499–386 BC*. Essential Histories 36. Oxford: Osprey Publishing.

A close-up of a Persian guard, the relief carved in Persepolis during the time of Xerxes. In addition to his leaf-bladed spear, this warrior has a composite bow slung over his shoulder, with the *gorytos* quiver on his back. Note the highly curved bow tips, a characteristic of many Persian bows. (Photo by Roger Viollet/Getty Images)

INDEX

References to illustrations are shown in **bold**.

Achaean/Aetolain forces 41, 72–73
Aeginetan/Ambraciot forces **59**, 62
Alexander III of Macedon 26, 74, **75**, 75
Amompharetus 58, 63, 64
Anactorian/Arcadian forces 43, **59**, 61, 62
archers (Grk) 26, 58, 60, 72
archers (Per) **16**, **17**, 26, 27, 28, 35, 36, 37, 50:
    clothing 37; equipment **15**, **16**, **17**, 22, **23**,
    28, **37**, 79; use in combat 27, 37, 38, 44,
    48–49, 52, **66–67**, 71
Artabazus 64, 76
Artemisium, battle of (480 BC) 54
Athenian forces **10**, **11**, 12–13, 31, 56, 58, **59**,
    60, 62, **66–67**, 73
    use in combat 32, **33**, 36, 37, 38, 65, **66–67**,
    69, 73
Athens (Persian threat to) 30, 32, 34, 38, 42,
    54, 55, 56, 57

Bactrian forces **59**, 60
battle-axes 23, **48–49**, 55, **66–67**
battlefield communications 14, 25, 27–28, 70
    messengers/runners (Grk) 25, 40
Boeotia (Greek/Persian forces in) 54, 57
Boeotian forces 31, 41, 43
bows and arrows 5: (Grk) 18, 60; (Per) 14,
    15, **16**, 17, **17**, 18, 22–23, **23**, 26, 27, 28,
    35, 36, 37, **37**, 39, 46, 50, 52, 55, 58, 62,
    64, 65, **66–67**, 79

Carian/Cephallenian forces 23, 62
cavalry forces (Grk) 9, 12, 74, 75
cavalry forces (Per) 6, **14**, 15, 23, 26, 27, 28,
    30, 34, **59**, 60
    clothing 23, 60
    headgear 23
    use in combat 27, 58, **59**, 60, 62, 64, 65,
    66–67, 69, 71, 72
        battle tactics **66–67**, 69
    weaponry 22, 23, 27, 58, 62, 65, **66–67**
Chalcidian forces 41, **59**, 62
charioteers/chariots 6, 27, **27**, 31
Corinth, battle of (392 BC) 73
Corinthian forces 43, **59**, 61
Cunaxa, battle of (401 BC) 73
Cyrus the Great 8, 26, 27, 29, 78

Darius I 6, 7, 16, 29, 30, **30**, 41, 42, 53, 57, 77
Datis 7, 30, 34, 35
Delian League 76, 77
Delium, battle of (424 BC) 24

Enienes/Eordi forces 41
Ephialtes (treachery of) 44, 46, 50, 51
Epidaurian forces **59**
Eretria (Persian conquest of) 7, 29, 30, 31
Eretrian forces **59**, 62
Ethiopian forces 23
Eurymedon, battle of (469/466 BC) 76

Greek armies
    battle formations/tactics 4, 13, 24–26, 32,
    33, 35–36, 64, 73–75
        othismos ('push') 5, 24–26, 27, 37,
        69, 71
        phalanx 5, 10, 12, 24–26, 27, 28, 35,
        36–37, **36**, 38, **48–49**, 63, **66–67**, 69,
        70–72, **72**
        shield wall 28, **57**, 58, **66–67**, **74**
    composition/organization 26, 78
        and Greek class structure 12
        Iphicratean reforms 71, 73
        standing armies (*poleis*) 8, 9, 12, 24, 29, 71
        'tribal' regiments **10**, **11**, 12, 35–36,
        37, 78

Greek hoplites 6, 12, 26, **40**, 71, 73, 74
    armour/body protection **9**, **10**, **11**, 18, 20,
    21, **24**, 28, 47, 51, 69, 73
    clothing/dress **10**, **11**, 43, 51, 69
    equipment 13, 18, 19–21, 24, **24**, 25, **25**,
    36, **40**, 43, 47, 64, 69, **72**, 74
    headgear **9**, **10**, **11**, 18, 21, **24**, 35, **39**, **40**,
    47, 51, 69
    training/military service **9**, **10**, 12–13
    use in combat 5, 25, **25**, 31, 32, 33, 35,
    36–38, **39**, 43, 52, 57, 61, 65, 71,
    72–73, **74**
    weaponry 5, **9**, **10**, **11**, 12, 13, 17, 18,
    19–21, **19**, 24, **24**, 25, **25**, 31, 36, **39**, 43,
    47, 64, 74
Greek naval forces/vessels 9, 12, 29, 54

Hellenic League 42, 54, 76
Hermonian forces **59**, 62

Indian forces **59**, 60
Ionian Revolt (499–494 BC) 7, 29–30, 31, 57
Issus, battle of (333 BC) 77

javelin men/javelineers 6, 12, 26, 27, 72–73
javelins 5: (Grk) 18, 73; (Per) 14, 18, 23, 27,
    58, 62, 65, **66–67**

Lacedaemonian forces 29, 50, 53, **59**, 60–61,
    65, 70, 73
Lade, battle of (494 BC) 30
Leonidas I (Spartan king) 42, 43, 44, 46, 51,
    51, 52, 53, 56
Lepran/Leucadian forces **59**, 61, 62
Lydian forces 23

Macedonia (Persian forces in) 30, 42
Macedonian forces 41, 74
Magnesian/Mantinean forces 41, 74
Marathon, battle of (490 BC) 7, **7**, 33, **38**, **40**
    composition/disposition of forces **10**, **11**,
    16, **17**, 29–31, 32, **32**, 33, 34, 35–36,
    36, 71–72
    nature of combat 32, 36–38, **36**, 40
Mardonius 56–57, 60, 62, 64, 69, 75
Masistius 58, 60
Median forces **18**, 26, 36, 46, **59**, 60
Medizing Greeks **59**, 60, 65
Megarian forces 58, **59**, 60, 62
Miltiades 31, 34–35
Mycale, battle of (479 BC) 76
Mycenaean forces 43, **59**, 61

Naxos (Persian conquest of) 7, 31

Paeonian forces 41, 73
Palean forces **59**
Parthian forces 23
Pausanias 56, 57, 60, 61, 62, 65, 75
Peloponnesian War (431–404 BC) 26,
    72–73, 77
peltasts 71, 73
Perrhaebi/Phikian forces 41, 42
Persian armies
    battle formations/tactics 6, 26–28, **48–49**,
    66–67, 71–72
    composition/organization 8, **18**, 14, 23, 26,
    27, 35, 41–42, 78
Persian Empire (composition/extent) 7, **7**, 8,
    29, 30, 74–77
Persian fleets/vessels 7, 30, 31, 32, 38, 41, 42,
    54, 56, 57
Persian Immortals 8, **23**, 26, **26**, 44, **45**, 46,
    50–51, 52
Persian warriors 30, 58
    armour/body protection 6, 14, 15, 17, **17**,
    18, 22, 28, **43**, 60, **66–67**, 69

clothing/dress 14, 15, 17, 22, 28, **43**
equipment 22–23, **23**, 28, 36, **48–49**,
    66–67, 79
footwear **16**, 17
headgear **16**, **17**, 18, 22
training/military service 14–15, 18
use in combat 6, 15, 17, 22, 26–27, 28, 32,
    33, 36–38, 36, 43, 44, **48–49**, 53, 64,
    66–67, 69, 71
weaponry 6, 27, 22–23, **23**, 28, 36, **43**,
    48–49, 53, 64, **66–67**, 79
Philip II of Macedon 26, 74
Phleiasian forces **59**; Phlius forces 42, 62
Phocian forces 43, 44, 45, 50–51
Plataea, battle of (479 BC)
    composition/disposition of forces 54, **55**,
    56–57, 58, **59**, **59**, 60–64, 72
    nature of combat 6, 57, 58, 60, 62–65,
    66–67, 69, 75
Plataean forces 31, 34, **36**, 37, 56, **59**, 62
polemarches 31, 34, 63, 73
Potidaean forces **59**, 61

sabres: (Grk) **22**, **43**; (Per) 15, 43, 55
Sacae forces **59**, 60
Salamis, battle of (480 BC) 56
Samos (Persian conquest of) 31
Sardis 30, 41, 42
Scythian archers **16**, **17**, 18, 23, 35, 55
shields (Grk) 5, **9**, 13, 18, 19, 21, 24, 25, 28,
    36, 46, **48–49**, 65, 69, **72**, 74, **74**
    decoration/motifs **10**, **11**, 43, **72**
    elements/features of **10**, **11**, 20–21, **25**, 47,
    63, 68
    types **25**: *aspis* **10**, **11**, 20–21, 24, **40**, 43,
    47, 51, 57, 63, **66–67**, 71, 73; *hoplon* **10**,
    11; *pelte* 71, 73
shields (Per) 6, 15, 18, 22, 23, 24, 26, 28, 36,
    37, **48–49**, **66–67**
Sicyonian forces **59**, 61
slingers/slings 5, 12, 18, 26
Sparta 9, 24, 29, 30, 42, 56, 77
Spartan warriors 9, 13, 24, **25**, 43, 51, **51**, 56,
    59, 61, 69, 70, 75
    use in combat **24**, 26, 34, 38, 42, 43, 44,
    45, 46, **48–49**, 50, 51–52, 58, 63, 64, 65,
    66–67, 69, 72, 73
spears (Grk) 5, 13, **13**, 17, **19**, 28, 36, **39**, **40**,
    46, 47, 52, 65, 73, 74: *dory* **10**, **11**, **19**, 25,
    31, **48–49**, **66–67**
spears (Per) 5, **14**, 15, **15**, 18, 22, 23, **23**, 26,
    28, 36, 37, 55, 64, **66–67**, 79
strategio 12, 31, 34–35
Styrian forces **59**, 62
swords (Grk) 13, 17, 18, 21, **24**, 25, 37, 51,
    65, 73: *falchion* 21; *kopis* 21, 23, 28;
    machiara 21; *xiphos* **10**, **11**, **19**, 21, **24**, 28,
    48–49, 64
swords (Per) 6, 18, 21, 26, 27, 36, 37, 64,
    66–67: *akenakes* 28
Syracusan troops 25

Tegean forces 43, **59**, 61, 62, 65, 69
Theban forces 24, 51, 43, 44, 52, 76
Thebes 12, 76
Thermopylae, battle of (480 BC)
    composition/disposition of forces 41–43, 44,
    44, **45**, 46, 50–51, 52, 71–72
    nature of combat 26, 44, 46, **48–49**, 50–53
Thespian forces 43, 44, 51, 52, **59**
Thessaly (Persian forces in) 42, 56
Thrace (Persian forces in) 29, 42
Thracian forces 31, 41, 71, 73
Tirynthian/Troezenian forces **59**, 61

Xerxes I 28, 41, 42, 46, 50, 51, 52–53, 54, 56,
    57, 76, 77, **77**, 79